Marketing Matters

A MARKET ANALYSIS METHODOLOGY LEADING
TO A MARKETING SIMULATION CAPABILITY

KENDALL CAREY

Archway Publishing books may be ordered through booksellers or by contacting:

Archway Publishing
1663 Liberty Drive
Bloomington, IN 47403
www.archwaypublishing.com
1 (888) 242-5904

Because of the dynamic nature of the Internet, any web addresses or links contained in this book may have changed since publication and may no longer be valid. The views expressed in this work are solely those of the author and do not necessarily reflect the views of the publisher, and the publisher hereby disclaims any responsibility for them.

Any people depicted in stock imagery provided by Getty Images are models, and such images are being used for illustrative purposes only. Certain stock imagery © Getty Images.

ISBN: 978-1-4808-8934-7 (sc)
ISBN: 978-1-4808-9062-6 (hc)
ISBN: 978-1-4808-9063-3 (e)

Library of Congress Control Number: 2020909618

Print information available on the last page.

Archway Publishing rev. date: 06/02/2020

CONTENTS

INTRODUCTION

Marketing Matters provides a methodology for the marketing function within an organization from market analysis through to simulation modelling of different possible market outcomes. It is possible to do this because of a tool, the Carey Price Sensitivity Curve, that allows the price sensitivity of the market to be measured. This curve shows the importance of price relative to everything else in any properly defined product or service market segment, which is defined as a group of buyers with approximately the same need profile within a particular piece of geography.

The need profiles of segments are approximated using weights representing the relative importance of different needs, with the most important non-price need being given a weight of 100, to which all the other needs are related based on their relative importance to the buyers. If a need is half as important as the most important need it is given a weight of 50.

Having established the need profile for the segment, the performance of each competitor is rated relative to the need weight. If a need is being fully satisfied by a company, that company is given a performance rating equal to the need weight. Each company active in the segment is rated relative to each need and their total ratings, including price, are expressed as a percentage of the sum total of all the segment ratings; these percentages are the equivalent of market segment shares.

The analysis can then be used to determine what changes need to be made in order to improve market performance and the cost of these changes can be estimated, to determine whether or not an action is worth taking, based on the change in profitability resulting from the combination of the change in market share, and hence volume, with the changes in the costs of taking the action.

This results in a hierarchy of possible actions from the most profitable down to the least profitable from which can be selected the actions with the highest probability of increasing profitability.

A further step, if desired, would be to estimate what the competitive reactions would be over time and hence what the net result would be for a given period of time in terms of profitability. This then allows the net effect on profitability to be estimated for any slate of actions both by our own company and by our competitors or, in other words, to simulate the financial impact of any course of action.

CHAPTER 1   SEGMENTATION: THE KEY TO ALL MARKETING

One of the best definitions of segmentation as it applies in business to business (B2B) marketing is that used by Aubrey Wilson in his book, "The Assessment of Industrial Markets". He defines segmentation as:

"The division of large disparate markets into smaller homogeneous segments each with one or several common characteristics."

A *market* can be segmented in a wide variety of different ways. Any division can be made based on any characteristic or variable of interest. For example: the automobile market could theoretically be segmented on the basis of purchasers' preferences for chicken soup. Now, while it might be intriguing to know that Honda drivers are twice as keen on chicken soup as Buick drivers, this information could only be of interest to trivia buffs or a frustrated copy writer in an advertising agency. On the other hand, if the market for automobiles is segmented by color preference and price sensitivity, this would have obvious utility to the automobile manufacturers in determining what to make and how to price it. Thus, segmentation is not simply a matter of preference, and different types of segmentation vary in their utility, some being essential to any rational attempt at marketing and others being largely irrelevant.

Since we are concerned here with industrial and B2B marketing, we fortunately do not have to bother as much as consumer marketers do with measurability, accessibility, or the ability to direct one's marketing efforts at a particular segment. For example: through product research and product experimentation, we discover that there exists a segment of beer drinkers who prefer a combination of low alcohol, light taste, and a designer bottle. We do not necessarily know how many there are, how much they drink, or most importantly, how to reach them, unless they are clearly defined by a combination of some other characteristics such as income, education, or profession. Even then, they may be hard to communicate with vis a vis beer. In industrial markets, it is generally possible to find ways of measuring market segments once they have been identified, since the companies that comprise each segment are identified in the segmentation process as being a certain size, in a particular industry, serving a specific market, etc. They are therefore accessible through a wide variety of directories, and if required, field work research can be used to establish their usage of a product or service. So in industrial marketing, we can concentrate on segmenting markets in a useful way without being unduly constrained by concerns about measurability and accessibility.

What then is the point of segmentation and how should it be done? To answer this question, the reason for segmenting is to be able to run a business better; to make it more productive and efficient in the ways it satisfies its customers' requirements. The types of segmentation that help in this respect are product segmentation, geographic segmentation and segmentation based on customer needs. However, as will be seen, in order to be useful, the segmentation must be done in very specific ways

1.1   Product Segmentation

The first and most obvious thing we need to know in order to improve our business is which products or services are making money and which aren't, since profitability tends to be product or service related. Most companies have no problem with this in principle, but many do not classify or identify product lines appropriately to yield useful information. A product line should be segmented based on the following:

- the equipment used to produce it
- differences in variable costs of production

- differences in efficiency of production
- differences in price

If there are significant differences in any of the above, then the products should be differentiated and the size of their markets should be measured for whatever geographic areas are of interest to the business. This yields invaluable information concerning not only the profitability of particular product lines but also the company's share of the market and hence a rough measure of the product's potential. Depending on the company's circumstances, even this limited information may inspire action. If the company is running at full capacity, then some product rationalization may be desirable. If more sales are needed, it suggests some directions in which to generate more profitable business.

Unfortunately, many companies do not segment their product line properly, or if they do, they do not bother to find out how big the markets for them are. The reasons can vary from lack of resources and poor cost accounting to unnecessary complexity and bad management. An example of unnecessary complexity is to divide the market into too many product subgroups based on minor technical differences. This is particularly common in capital-intensive and production-oriented businesses, like pulp and paper.

If a business is complex, then that complexity must be accepted and dealt with rationally. Attempts to artificially simplify a business by aggregation of data will not lead to elegant solutions but to an Alice in Wonderland world of total confusion. The aggregation disguises the real differences in the costs, pricing and profitability of different products. Ignoring these differences is like choosing to drive a car in a fog or whiteout rather than on a clear day.

1.2   Geographic Segmentation

Geographic segmentation is important from two perspectives. First, the impact on profitability of shipping product great distances is dramatic in many industries. Second, the competition, both their identities and their numbers, will usually vary geographically, although this is less true for products or services that are primarily delivered online.

Amongst the industries in which shipping costs are very important are pulp and paper, mining, cement, and chemicals. In each case, the mode and distance of deliveries dramatically impacts the bottom line, so that companies stay as close to "home" as possible. Because of this, the geographic reach of companies with relatively high freight costs relative to their margins varies depending on the supply/demand balance. In times of excess supply, the "acceptable" shipping area grows, whereas when there is excess, demand in that shipping area shrinks.

The second reason for geographic segmentation, namely the identities and numbers of competitors, results in different geographic areas being relevant in different businesses. In most retail businesses, the relevance of geography is determined by customer perceptions of convenience, which vary with the nature of the product. For example, most buyers of gasoline will not typically deviate from their route to fill up with gas unless there is a special incentive or an emergency. The competition is therefore defined by the distance someone is prepared to travel having decided they need to fill up. Typically, this is not more than a mile or two, so that retail gas competition is clustered around major intersections with that kind of radius.

On the other hand, for important works of art, the entire world is the market because buyers will come to the source of the unique offering. Thus, the value of the product or service tends to define how far people are prepared to go to take advantage of a product offering or how much they are prepared to pay to have it brought to them.

For any given product or service, geography typically defines the competition. The same performance in terms of quality, service and price in different areas may result in dramatic differences in market share or profitability because of the performance of the competition.

Geographic or competitive segmentation is not difficult to understand conceptually and does not require further elaboration except to illustrate how the competition varies in many businesses, depending on the stage of the economic cycle, or the supply/demand balance. In boom times, when industrial or capital-intensive companies reach full capacity, they tend to pull back to a smaller shipping area where their costs are lowest. In recessions, they expand their reach in order to increase sales. Thus, the boundaries of geographic segments may vary with economic conditions. The effect of this (illustrated in Diagram 1) is that all the segments grow in size in recessions because the geographic boundaries of the segments change. Segment 1 in which companies with production facilities at A and B compete and Segment 3 in which companies producing at C and D compete, both expand. At the same time, the size of Segment 2 increases in which all the companies compete. Similar effects will occur on the other boundaries, if there are other competitors in those areas.

Diagram 1

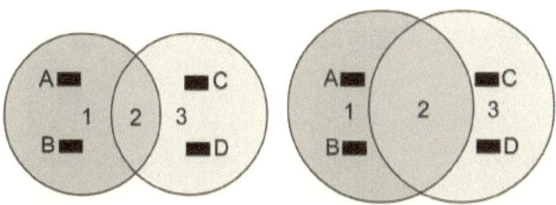

The impact of these segment changes is increased dramatically if there are barriers limiting the expansion, such as oceans or other national boundaries as illustrated in Diagram 2.

DIAGRAM 2

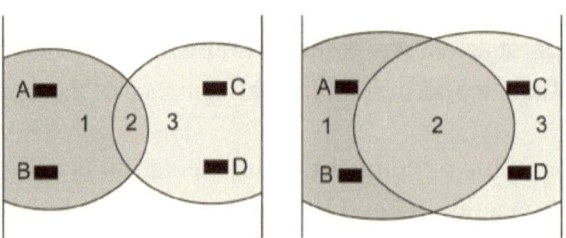

Changes in tariffs and shipping modes can also heavily impact geographic segmentation through affecting the number and identities of competitors in different areas, thereby redefining the segment borders.

1.3   Customer Need or Market Segmentation

The third type of segmentation that is vital to any segmentation analysis is segmentation based on customers' needs, which hereafter will be referred to as market segmentation. In the case of market segmentation, each segment will be only approximately homogeneous in terms of needs. The amount of variability that can be accepted is partly a matter of judgement and indeed the whole subject of market segmentation is infinitely more complex than product or geographic segmentation. For this reason, the subject is discussed at length in the next chapter, but before embarking on that topic, it may be useful to briefly review some ways of segmenting markets that surprisingly are commonly used, but in most cases are relatively ineffective.

1.4   Types of Unproductive Segmentation

Commonly used but generally unproductive ways of segmenting markets include geographic segmentation related to office locations or political boundaries, segmentation based on industry or end use, segmentation by customer and segmentation by broad product groupings, each of which is discussed below. Generally, these ways of segmenting a market tell us nothing useful about the market per se but rather are convenient breakdowns for administrative, accounting, sales or statistical reasons. Segmenting markets in these ways generally leads to a dead end, that is, nothing can be done with the information other than to say, as older readers may remember Arte Johnson saying in his German soldier role on "Laugh-In", "ver-r-ry interesting but stupid".

For example: segmenting a market *geographically* according to political or administrative convenience is only of use if, fortuitously, differences in customer needs correspond with the geographic boundaries, the competition is different in one area versus another, or distribution costs are congruous with the geographic areas. In the first case, the actions available to a supplier may be numerous in terms of better satisfying the customer needs; in the second case, further analysis can yield useful performance data vis a vis the competition in one area compared with another; in the third case, profitability is consistent with the geographic boundaries. If none of these situations prevail, geographic segmentation is meaningless. If however, the geographic segments fortuitously are meaningful, why not set out to segment on the basis of customer needs, competition or profitability in the first place?

Segmentation based on *industry* identity or end use can have value, where products are designed for an application peculiar to a particular industry, but even in these cases, there are likely to be market segments within an industry which better define customers' needs. For example: the chemical industry contains a multitude of segments within the market for a single product, which are determined by such variables as customer size, the markets served, and the end product value. For most products, industry segmentation is meaningless except possibly as a guide to future growth. However, even in this instance, there are likely to be significant differences in growth rates between one part of an industry and another based on the product line being produced or geographical factors.

Segmentation by *customer* is often cited as being the ultimate in industrial segmentation and may well have been the motivation for supply chain, or value chain analysis, in which a company's major customers are dissected in order to determine how they add value and hence what factors a supplier should be cognizant of in developing an offering. There are three problems with this approach.

The first is that large customers tend to be participants in a number of different markets or to be involved in a number of different businesses and thus are heterogeneous in their needs. They in effect may seem to behave in schizophrenic ways depending on which of their market segments or businesses is the largest or is currently of most concern. Secondly, if they are indeed a very homogeneous business i.e. a simple product line serving very few market segments, they are unlikely to be big enough to warrant the type of individual attention required in a value chain analysis or the special treatment to which such an analysis might point. Under these circumstances, like businesses need to be grouped into segments in order to determine what should or should not be done to satisfy their requirements. Finally, and most importantly, a concentration on large customers will allow the smaller but rapidly growing customers to be neglected, and they more often than not represent the supplying company's future prospects.

Segmenting by *broad product groupings* is also problematic. For example: if we were segmenting our paper business and referred to "Fine Papers" which includes all types of woodfree printing and writing papers, we would be combining a wide variety of products that are made on different machines, have different costs, serve different markets, have different prices and vary widely in their profitability. Thus, a statement such as "Our North American Fine Paper Business Improved its Market Share and Earnings" may be accepted as an annual report summary, but actually communicates nothing of consequence by way of a real explanation of the company's performance. It is the business equivalent of saying "our family grew six inches last year".

Thus, each of these ways of segmenting a market may have utility but only under special sets of circumstances. A better approach than segmenting for convenience is to base market segmentation on why it is necessary in the first place, that is, in order to run a better business through understanding and satisfying customer needs profitably.

If the segmentation is done as has been suggested earlier, that is, by product, geography and market (homogeneous customer needs), then a company's business can be perceived as a three-dimensional matrix of segments as shown in Diagram 3.

DIAGRAM 3

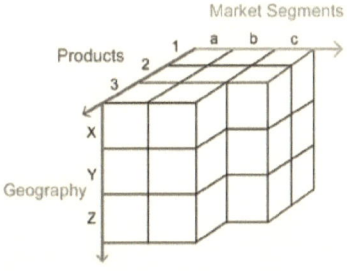

This matrix can then be used to identify the segments of most interest and to determine a company's strategic direction. How this can be done is discussed in Chapter 5, but first it is necessary to ensure that the market segmentation is both clearly understood and correctly done in practice.

CHAPTER 2   MARKET SEGMENTATION BASED ON NEEDS

Market segmentation originated in consumer marketing, when it was recognized that individual consumers differed in their desires or expectations with respect to products and services. Clearly for most products and services, it was impractical to attempt to satisfy each individual with respect to their specific needs so they were grouped into more or less homogeneous bunches and called segments. So we end up with segments being identified by the dominant behavior characteristic(s) or behavior patterns such as price conscious, image conscious, taste conscious, etc. or what is believed to cause their likes or dislikes in terms of measurable attributes such as socio-economic status or nationality. However, knowing that people differ in their needs is not very useful to potential suppliers unless they know how many people comprise each segment and their consumption rate i.e. how large is each segment.

As long as segments are differentiated by readily measurable characteristics available in census or other data, then their size or potential size can be measured. However, when the differentiating factors are not as easily measured, market research has to be used to determine the size of the various segments using such techniques as multi-dimensional scaling. These allow the relative importance of a variety of needs related to a product or service to be evaluated relative to each other for a given sample of users; they also measure the size of each grouping of users in each segment. Segmentation therefore became a very powerful tool in consumer marketing by allowing a supplier to pick the segments in which he or she wished to participate and then to package the product or service offering appropriately for each segment.

The relevance of segmentation to industrial businesses varies depending upon the number of actual and potential accounts a business has to deal with. If they are very few, then each customer could be dealt with individually although, as has been mentioned, each could participate in a number of segments. However, if there are many, i.e. more than 30, then market segmentation will certainly be a good idea, since it is very difficult to deal with more than 30 different ways of handling clients without causing administrative and organizational confusion. Where the number of accounts is small and each account is relatively homogeneous, i.e. is not involved in a wide variety of different businesses, then the "value chain" or "supply chain" approach can be used effectively on its own; otherwise segmentation is necessary.

2.1   B2B Market Segmentation

So what is different about B2B marketing segmentation compared with consumer marketing segmentation? Firstly, an industrial customer or potential customer is not an individual but an organization, and a variety of people or functions may contribute to the decision to purchase a particular product or service. Secondly, the number of product or service attributes that may be taken into account is generally much greater than for consumer products. Finally, even if you know who participates in the decision and the decision criteria for a particular organization, how do you recognize which company belongs in which segment in order to determine how large the segments are? These factors combine to make B2B market segmentation a particularly difficult exercise, which helps to explain why, despite all the lip service given to adopting "marketing" thinking in industrial corporations, so few industrial companies actually practice marketing. Segmentation is, after all, the key to applying the marketing principle of need satisfaction, while making a healthy profit; if the needs are not known or the different needs of various segments are ignored, then need satisfaction is entirely fortuitous, if it occurs at all.

Another reason industrial companies have been slower in adopting marketing driven policies is the perceived difficulty of responding to the various different needs of each segment when they are known. For example, some products which are produced in large, Capital-Intensive facilities to a given specification cannot readily be varied - it is simply impractical in many cases to alter the specification to suit different segments. However, this constraint does not normally apply to the service components of customers' needs such as delivery and technical service, and even if it is impractical to vary the product for different segments, it is nevertheless a good idea to understand how much potential business you may be foregoing by failing to do so.

2.2   B2B Market Segmentation Theory

As is the case in consumer marketing, it is nearly impossible to make sense of segmentation in B2B markets unless the segments are specifically identified with a product or service. A buyer's needs related to say, office furniture, will have nothing to do with the same buyer's needs related to robotics or paper supplies. Segmentation for some products will tend to result from the type of business or industry a potential customer is in. For example: the computer needs of financial institutions will be quite different from those of a mining company. This type of segmentation tends therefore towards being *vertical*, i.e. the segments tend to align with industries such as "the foundry industry", "banking" or "telecommunications", or with parts of an industry defined by the type of product it produces or the type of service it provides.

For other products such as office furniture, segmentation is related to function, i.e. a production office, an accounting office, or a President's office, or possibly to company size, rather than to the industry or the type of business. This is referred to as *horizontal* segmentation because it cuts across industry boundaries. For example: in the case of the computer needs of financial institutions, the transaction-based computer needs of *small* financial institutions are likely to differ from those of *large* financial institutions, even though they are in precisely the same business, because they will have fewer branches, fewer accounts and fewer transactions to cope with.

Seldom, however, is the real market segmentation for a product or service either totally vertical or totally horizontal. There will in some cases be vertical or horizontal subdivisions and in others, vertical or horizontal groupings. An example of a vertical subdivision relative to computer software, would be the distinction between large *domestic* financial institutions, and large *international* financial institutions. Each will have different software requirements for transfers of assets. An example of a horizontal subdivision would be differentiating within large financial institutions between *consumers* and *businesses* as the markets served. Again, their software requirements would differ. It is thus extremely important that prior to attempting market segmentation, the product or service be clearly identified.

As was discussed in Chapter 1, the product or service under consideration determines costs, pricing, and capacity, so in order to use segmentation to generate profit related plans, the segments identified must be related to a product or service. It is therefore fortuitous that the product or service differentiation is also valuable in helping define market or need related segments.

2.3   Vertical and Horizontal Segmentation

Since we have defined vertical market segmentation as being that associated with different industries or subsections thereof, the ultimate vertical segmentation would be on a product by product basis. That is, we would subdivide industries into the specific products they produce. However, unless the needs generated by the manufacture of each product differ, the subdivision cannot be considered market segments otherwise we have *reductio ad absurdum*, i.e. in the fastener business, it makes no sense to differentiate down to the sizes of screws since the needs of a screw manufacturer will not differ with the size of the screw. Nevertheless, a single firm may manufacture several different products and therefore could be a participant, from a supplier's perspective, in several market segments. Our objective then, in order to identify *useful* vertical segments is to combine them as far as is practical into more or less homogeneous market segments defined in terms of needs. The mechanism that we can use to accomplish this is horizontal segmentation, which may be caused by a number of different factors. For example: company size may differentiate companies in terms of their needs for a product or service. Other possible horizontal segmentation causes or, as they are sometimes referred to, drivers, are as follows:

- how a product is used
- the markets served by a product or service
- competitive pressures
- cyclicality
- product complexity
- the relative value of the product purchased to that sold
- cultural influences
- degree of specialization in a product
- impact on productivity
- capital, labor or technology intensity
- testing capability or quality control

Which of these is relevant in segmenting the market for a particular product or service can generally be discerned from a review of the composition of the Decision Making Unit.

2.4 The Decision Making Unit (DMU)

For any given product or service, the needs of customers will result from the values of the people involved in the purchasing decision, each of whom will have a different functional responsibility. This mix of functional responsibilities and their relative importance we refer to as the Decision Making Unit (DMU).

The DMU comprises everybody whose input is used in deciding what to buy and from whom. This may include people from all of the following functions: general management, technical or product design experts, marketing, sales, production, accounting, maintenance, engineering, and purchasing or only a few of them, depending upon the product or service. The DMU may also include participants from a variety of organizations. For example: the DMU for industrial lighting can include any or all of the following functions from different companies: architect, electrical or lighting consultant, electrical contractor, and end user.

An example of a DMU and the nature of each function's involvement is outlined below for titanium dioxide. Titanium dioxide, a white powder, is used in the manufacture of high-quality printing and writing papers, paints and plastics in order to provide brightness and/or increased opacity. It is one of the most expensive additives in most products, but it is also very effective.

If we look at the paper industry, a potential supplier's product is initially tested by the laboratory of the Product Design function against a set of specifications and if found to be satisfactory, will be tried in production tests. Again, if found satisfactory, the supplier will be approved for use in certain grades of paper. At this stage, the choice or choices of supplier will be influenced by the various functions as follows:

The DMU and its Interests in Titanium Dioxide

Function in Customer's Business	Interest

Technical Product Design — The degree to which each supplier meets certain quality criteria and their product's consistency in color, brightness, particle size, particle shape, etc. is how this function evaluates suppliers. Each supplier's performance in these respects determines the basis for approval or rejection of individual shipments and also provides a quality track record.

Production — The ease of use and runability on the paper machines i.e. packaging and dispersion characteristics, as well as delivery service capability, technical service capability, and cost per ton of good paper.

Marketing and Sales — Paper product characteristics i.e. brightness, smoothness, opacity, color.

Accounting and Treasury — Cost per ton of paper produced and payment terms.

Purchasing — Cost per unit, reliability of supplies, supplier administration of orders and contract maintenance, flexibility in the scheduled quantities, inventory back-up, terms of sale, payment terms, quantity discounts, price.

General Management — All of the above plus security of supply, contract terms, and contract duration.

While this may seem somewhat complex, it is not particularly unusual for an industrial consumable which has a significant influence on product quality. However, it contrasts dramatically with the DMU for some other products such as paper clips, for which the DMU is probably either the purchasing agent or the individual responsible for office supplies who would have total responsibility for the choice of supplier.

The DMU will also be different if the relative importance of a function is different. That is, if production is more important in the decision re. purchasing Product A than the marketing function and the opposite is true for Product B, then these constitute different DMUs even though the people may be the same.

If we now return to the titanium dioxide example, we can look at the other user industries' DMUs to see if they differ from paper.

The various roles and influences of the DMU in the paper industry would be very similar, in fact, to those for paints and plastics, but there are differences in the DMU for different companies, resulting not from industry differences, but from the differences in the markets served, e.g. the business versus consumer markets for paint, or in the capital intensity of a producer. In the first case, that is the industrial versus consumer markets for paint, the role of the marketing people in the DMU is likely to be less pronounced for the business market and that of production and purchasing greater.

In the capital intensity example, the role of production will tend to be greater in a capital-intensive business and greater emphasis will be placed on product consistency, technical service and delivery service than in a less capital-intensive environment. The segment matrix might therefore be as shown in Table 1 in which each numeral identifies a segment.

TABLE 1			
POSSIBLE MARKET SEGMENTS FOR TITANIUM DIOXIDE			
	Vertical	Paper	Paint and Plastics
Horizontal			
Consumer	Capital-Intensive	NA	2
	Non Capital-Intensive	NA	3
Business	Capital-Intensive	1	1
	Non Capital-Intensive	NA	3
NA- Not Applicable			

In this example we have, so far, not found segment differences vertically, that is all three industries can, for segmentation purposes, be lumped together. However, it is also possible that one or more of the industries may contain sub-segments based upon the value of the end product being produced; that is, a segment producing high value products might have lower price sensitivity than a low product value segment. If this distinction applied to all the industries then it could be treated as a horizontal differentiator as shown in Table 2, but if it only applied to one industry, say plastics, then it would be treated as a vertical differentiator as shown in Table 3.

TABLE 2			
	Vertical		Paper, Paint & Plastics
Horizontal			
Consumer	High Value Product	Capital-Intensive	1
		Non Capital-Intensive	2
	Low Value Product	Capital-Intensive	3
		Non Capital-Intensive	4
Business to Business	High Value Product	Capital-Intensive	5
		Non Capital-Intensive	6
	Low Value Product	Capital-Intensive	7
		Non Capital-Intensive	8

TABLE 3			
Horizontal	Vertical	Plastics	Paper, Paint & Plastics
		High Value Products	Low Value Products
Consumer	Capital-Intensive	1	3
	Non Capital-Intensive	2	4
B2B	Capital-Intensive	5	7
	Non Capital-Intensive	6	8

In either case, the segments are in effect the same, but in Table 3 the "labelling" (or identification of the segments) is more efficient and meaningful since it makes it clear that high value products are likely to be encountered only in the plastics industry.

It is interesting and instructive in this case to once again refer to the DMU and ask ourselves whether or not the DMU is the same for high value products and low value products. What we will find is that it *is* the same DMU in terms of functions, but that greater emphasis is placed on price in the low value segment. This is very helpful in trying to determine whether to look for vertical segmentation or horizontal segmentation since the functions within the DMU tend to be different for horizontal segmentation, while for vertical segmentation, the functions may be the same but the identity and importance of the specific needs will be different.

In order to further test this hypothesis and to further familiarize the reader with the DMU concept and its application, we will examine segmentation in some other businesses, namely lubricants, diesel fuel for commercial trucks, variable speed drives, and finally, office supplies.

Lubricants

In many modern production facilities, the demands made on some lubricants are extreme, owing to the speed of the equipment and its continuous operation, for example, engines and paper machines. Equally, the cost of inadequate lubrication can be very high, varying from very high maintenance costs and product defects to plant shutdown. For less arduous applications, a particular generic quality of lubricant may be specified. However, for very arduous applications, special proprietary lubricants are required which are judged not by specification but by performance. The DMU for performance lubricants would be similar to that shown below.

Function in Customer's Business	Interest
Production	Performance ratings, technical service, quality production
Maintenance	Frequency of replacement, wear characteristics, quantity consumed
Purchasing	Order replacement, price, delivery requirements
General Management	Any or all of the above, depending on the severity of the problem

However, in the case of less arduous applications where a standard for lubricant product quality has been set, the DMU would be quite different.

Functions in Customer's Business	Interest
Product testing	Conformance to specification
Purchasing	Contract price, delivery schedule

For small companies who do not have a test laboratory and whose applications are not arduous, the purchase decision will again be based more on performance than specification, but differences in performance will be harder to recognize.

Their DMU would resemble the following.

Function in Customer's Business	Interest
Production	Lubricant quality as determined by performance
Purchasing	Price, delivery

The segmentation matrix would therefore be as shown in Table 4.

TABLE 4 INDUSTRIAL LUBRICANTS		
	Vertical	All Industries
Horizontal		
Performance Buyers		1
Large Specification Buyers		2
Small Performance Buyers		3

The DMU for each segment is different which supports the horizontal segmentation hypothesis. However, in this case, a single customer may belong to both Segments 1 and 2 and will appear to have a split personality depending upon which segment's needs are being addressed. However, this complexity will not exist unless both segments are buying the same product line. In practice, the "performance" buyers are likely to use a different product line and there will be vertical segments based on the nature of the applications such as paper machines, compressors and pumps for which the DMU will be the same, but the requirements will differ. The segments would then be described as shown in Table 5.

TABLE 5				
STANDARD LUBRICANT SEGMENTS				
Horizontal	Vertical		All Industries	
Large Specification Buyers			1	
Small Specification Buyers			2	
PERFORMANCE LUBRICANTS SEGMENTS				
Horizontal	Vertical Paper Machines	Compressors	Rolling Mills	Others
Performance Buyers	1	2	3	4

Diesel Fuel for Trucks

Diesel fuel is sold in bulk to large fleets which have their own storage facilities and from service stations on the road to both fleets and owner-operators. Trucks will normally fill-up on the road at "card-locks" which are card-driven pumps or account number driven pumps. If we consider only the card-lock market and the a/c # market, and if we concentrate initially on large, long haul fleets, then the DMU becomes quite complex, involving company headquarters staff as well as truck drivers.

Function in Customer's Business	Interest
Operations Management	National or regional coverage, fuel efficiency and quality, accessibility or convenience of pumps, pump reliability,

	card reader efficiency, billing information and timing, pricing, personal supplier contact, contract duration
Accounting	Billing information, contract duration, accuracy and timeliness, price, payment terms, volume rebates
Truck Drivers	Convenience of facilities, mechanical and non-mechanical services, pump reliability, on-site personal contact, card-lock location information
General Management	Supplier contact, supplier plans, contract terms, price, plus any of the above of particular concern, e.g. billing procedures and geographical coverage

By comparison, the owner-operators are their own DMU. They differ from the fleets in a number of important respects such as:

- they buy on a "spot" basis, not by contract
- they have no contact with a suppliers' management
- their billing requirements are much simpler
- they judge suppliers by the service they receive at the pump sites and put much more emphasis on the quality of the facility and its range of services than do the fleet buyers.

There are also differences between the needs of fleets and owner-operators whose business is local and those in long distance haulage, with local operators not requiring the same on-site services or a national or regional network of sites, but often requiring both diesel and gasoline to be available.

The resultant matrix of segments is shown in Table 6.

Vertical		Long Haul	Short Haul
TABLE 6			
Horizontal			
Fleet	Diesel	1	2
	Mixed	NA	3
Owner-Operator	Diesel	4	5

Once again, these segments support the vertical/horizontal segmentation hypotheses, since the DMU is different for the horizontal segments and the importance of needs differs for the vertical segments.

Variable Speed (VFAC) Drives

A variable speed drive is a solid state or electronic electrical drive which allows a motor or series of motors to vary their speed without having to convert the electrical power to DC current or to mechanical power. In many applications, they are capable of significantly reducing power consumption and maintenance costs. The example below of a DMU concerns the installation of variable speed drives to control the speed of pumps in a chemical plant.

Function in Customer's Business	Interest
Production	Specification or performance required, quality evaluation, price, installation, technical service and training, power savings estimate
Maintenance	Maintenance savings and training
Engineering	As for production, but with emphasis on installation, price and performance capability

Purchasing	Administration of bids, price, and subsequent contract terms, savings estimate
General Management	All of the above or none depending on the cost of the equipment relative to the total capital budget and whether it is a maintenance or capital item

The DMU is likely to be very similar for large organizations in other industries, but the specific requirements of potential customers are likely to be different for different applications, that is, pumps versus rolling mills or paper machines. Many of these applications will be specific to an industry and even for common equipment such as fans and pumps, the particular needs of customers may well be related to the type of industry. Thus, vertical segmentation is probable for products of this type.

However, there is also likely to be some horizontal segmentation related to customer size. Specifically, many smaller companies may not have separate engineering or electrical engineering specialists and may therefore lack the technical expertise of the large companies. Thus, the DMU will be different as will the customers' needs. The segmentation diagram will therefore be as shown in Table 7.

TABLE 7 VARIABLE SPEED (VFAC) DRIVES					
Vertical Horizontal	Steel Industry	Paper Industry	Mining	Water Treatment	Printing
Large Companies	1	2	3	4	5
Small Companies			6	7	8

Office Supplies

Every business uses office consumables such as floppy disks, paper, printer cartridges, pads, pens, etc. These products are used in the same way by all consumers. It is therefore very unlikely that there will be any vertical segmentation. However, not all businesses buy these products in the same way, e.g. contract versus spot, and the needs do differ amongst users. For example: utilities tend to have a lot of customers and a relatively heavy administrative load where their own billings are related to consumption. They also buy a wide variety of products and services and tend to have relatively formal procedures for letting supply contracts. Under these circumstances, the ordering of office supplies tends to be centralized in the purchasing department, with other departments having some (often very limited) discretion to specify the type of product they want, but seldom if ever, the brand or the supplier. They will also typically be very price sensitive and may tender their business. The DMU and its concerns would therefore be approximately as follows:

Function in Customer's Business	Interest
User Department	Type of product
Purchasing	Type of product and brand, price, contract terms, delivery, quality, product range, type and frequency of supplier contact

Other large organizations may have a different DMU because, for example, they have many branch offices or plants and they are more concerned with service capability and do not tender. The users therefore would have more say in the choice of supplier and these buyers would be less price sensitive.

For smaller organizations, the absolute amount of money spent on office consumables may not justify special considerations and may be left to a more junior purchasing agent or administrative person. In this case, there may be a number of additional segments, depending on the freedom of action of the purchaser and their motivations; they may become more like individual consumers with some emphasizing convenience, others price, and still others personal "well-being".

This market would therefore segment as shown in Table 8.

TABLE 8 OFFICE PRODUCTS				
Horizontal	Vertical All Industries	Price Sensitive	Convenience	Service
Large Centralized	1			
Large Decentralized	2			
Small		3	4	5

The hypothesis, namely that if we have a difference in the composition of the DMU for various segments, we are likely to find that the segmentation drivers or causes are horizontal, while if the DMU is the same or very similar, but the relative importance of needs varies between segments, then the segmentation is likely to be vertical, does seem to apply to all these very different businesses.

The next chapter addresses how to do market segmentation in practice.

CHAPTER 3   PRACTICAL MARKETING SEGMENTATION TECHNIQUES

One major advantage that business to business marketers generally have over their consumer product counterparts is that their organization has direct contact with its customers - through its sales force, its distributors, customer service or technical service people. As a result, there exists in-house or available, a large pool of customer and market knowledge. This knowledge is typically only tapped on "special" occasions such as putting together budgets or business plans or investigating the potential for a new product. Sales and customer visit reports are certainly written but they seldom address directly the issues important to the segmentation process, and if they do, the information is filed away in a manner that makes collecting and analyzing the information very difficult. Because of this, organizations intent on doing segmentation or market analysis typically resort immediately to market research. While this writer would, in most circumstances, be a strong supporter of market research, experience shows that it is extremely difficult to use it as a segmentation tool in industrial markets without first developing some reasonable ideas about how the market may segment and why. The reasons for this lie partly in the complexity of most industrial DMUs and partly in the difficulty of getting from respondents in the field, measures of the importance of various possible needs to the business of the customer, because of the time required to do the interviewing and the reluctance of the key respondents to participate.

This is not to suggest that all respondents are incapable of being objective, but that their degree of objectivity varies in a way that cannot be tracked and thus invalidates the results of the research. Also, because of the complexity of the decision process, the number of interviews and the type of interview, i.e. more personal than telephone, good market research tends to be very expensive so there is a strong temptation to take short cuts which also reduces the validity of the results.

However, if the in-house knowledge pool can be tapped, which in most cases it can, then most of what would be found through market research can be accessed directly. The research can then be structured to test the hypotheses developed which can be done both more effectively and more cheaply than starting with a clean slate or some purely subjective notions.

The most efficient way of tapping in-house knowledge we have found is to organise workshops comprising no more than eight people knowledgeable about the markets to be analyzed. These people will typically be in sales, technical service, and customer service, and where appropriate, distribution. Management personnel can be included, provided that they are knowledgeable about the market and do not in any way intimidate or influence any of the other participants. It is also beneficial if the workshops are conducted off-site, both to minimise disruptions and to provide the appropriate neutral environment for dealing with an unfamiliar approach to looking at their business. The workshops should be led or conducted by an external consultant who understands industrial marketing and segmentation but has no strongly held opinions about the markets under review. Once the group is assembled, it can be told simply that the objective is to use their knowledge and experience in order to segment the market for whatever products are of interest, i.e. to divide up their customers and potential customers into more or less homogeneous groups in terms of the customer needs.

3.1   Segmentation Workshops

The first step using the workshop approach is to make a list of the specific "needs" of customers in general in the business being analyzed. The list will typically consist of a number of needs within each of the following categories. Some generic examples within each category are provided in Table 9.

TABLE 9
EXAMPLES OF CUSTOMER NEEDS

Need Category	Specific Needs
Product/Service	quality assurance, consistency, reliability, productivity
Delivery	JIT (just-in-time), weekly, when required
Technical Support/Service	technical advice, testing, equipment design and operation
Specific Support Services	product design, graphic design, product research, order processing efficiency
Administrative	invoicing, shipping documentation
Financial	credit terms, leasing
Policy	security of supply, policy consistency, environmental practices
Price	competitive price, contract price, quantity discount
Environmental	waste generation, toxicity, product handling, disposability

At this stage in the process, it is not important that the list be complete since other "needs" can be added later. However, it is very important that each need in the list be carefully defined and that any overlap or duplication be eliminated.

Having developed a reasonably comprehensive list of mutually exclusive needs, the next step is for a member of the group to identify a particular customer. Then the group selects the needs from the list (related to a particular product or service) which are applicable to this customer and adds any that are required, but not listed. It is often helpful to consider the composition of the DMU at this stage to ensure that no needs are missed.

The next step is to assign weights to the various needs, excluding the need for a low price. Generally, if price is not excluded then it proves difficult, if not impossible, to get the group to focus on the relative importance of each of the non-price needs. The weighting system can be whatever the group is comfortable with, but a system that assigns the most important "need" or "needs" a weighting of 100 and then relates the other needs to that (or those) seems to work well. Again, remembering who is involved in the DMU is useful in assigning the appropriate weights to the needs.

The assignment of weights is not necessarily an argument-free process, in fact, the initial efforts invariably result in conflict. This is generally the result of a misinterpretation of what is meant by a particular need but can also reflect genuine differences of opinion. However, rather than get bogged down in an attempt to resolve these early conflicts, it is more efficient to simply note the range of weights that have been suggested and move on to another customer. The second customer should be as different as possible from the first, except that they buy the same product, and the weighting procedure is repeated.

Two or three more customers can be dealt with until a fair degree of comfort is developed in the procedure and the results it produces. Typically after four or five customers have been analyzed, it is possible to resolve the differences that may have occurred initially because the comparison of the need weights of different customers makes clear that one or other point of view or a compromise position is in fact correct.

To illustrate how this works in practice, we will use examples from the corrugated case business. At this stage we would have developed customer specific need profiles which would look approximately as shown in Table 10.

TABLE 10
NEED PROFILES OF CORRUGATED CASE USERS

NEED	TYPE OF COMPANY				
	Beer Company	Power Tool Company	Winery	Chilled Meat Packer	Fresh Produce Producer
Carton Performance				100	100
Carton Specification	80	75	80		
Carton Design		80			60
Runability	90				
Graphic Design	20	85			50
Print Quality	80	100	100	40	60
Delivery Service	100	85	30	100	100
Emergency Delivery				10	
Administrative Service	40	35	30	20	60
Enquiry Response Time					20
Order Status Reports				30	
Technical Service	30				
Sales Contact	60	65	60	50	60
Confidentiality	80				
Credit					20
Management Contact	50	15			

1. Runability refers to the need for a corrugated case that runs efficiently through the container forming, filling and sealing line, i.e. it does not mis-form or jam the equipment.
2. Confidentiality is related to the need of this beer company for secrecy concerning its new brand positioning, launch dates, graphics, etc. to ensure that its competitor cannot undermine the effectiveness of the launch.

As is obvious, the need profiles are very different and would seem to indicate that these customers belong in different segments.

3.2   Segmentation Drivers

Our next objective is to determine what is causing the differences which are referred to as "drivers", i.e. is it the product they make (vertical segmentation), their size, the market served, or the degree of automation (horizontal segmentation). Listed below are the horizontal segmentation drivers that the author has come across, but there are doubtless others.

- the particular markets served, e.g. consumer, industrial, government or groupings within these categories
- the competitive pressures they are under or not under
- company size
- cyclicality i.e. how cyclical their business is
- the complexity of their business in terms of the number of products, transactions, accounts or suppliers
- the value of a product they buy relative to the value of what they sell
- cultural or religious differences
- degree of specialization in a product
- potential impact of a purchase on productivity
- capital, labor, or technology intensity

Typically, the group will suggest four or five factors that could be causing the segmentation and the product they produce. Vertical segmentation is invariably one of them. As far as the horizontal segmentation is concerned, the DMU is usually a good source of inspiration and guidance, especially for the relative importance of production, technical marketing and purchasing personnel. A DMU chart is shown in Table 11 for some corrugated case buyers.

TABLE 11
THE DMU

	Beer Company	Power Tool Company	Winery	Chilled Meat Packer	Fresh Produce Producer
Purchasing	X	X		X	
Production	X	X	X	X	X
Technical	X	X			
Marketing	X	X	X		X
General Management Or Owner			X		X

In this particular case, the horizontal drivers that seemed most likely to be at work were:

- degree of automation of assembly or filling operation because of the high weight for runability in only one instance (see Table 10).
- markets served, i.e. consumer vs industrial or commercial because of the differences in graphic design and print quality.
- company size because of the confidentiality need and the differences in the composition of the DMU between the winery and the beer company.

Starting with the "beer company", the group then thought of another beer company which was different in terms of size, i.e. small, and degree of automation (less automation and slower equipment). What they developed as a need profile is shown in Table 12 and also compared with the large beer company and the winery.

TABLE 12

	Large Automated Beer Company	Small, less Automated Beer Company	Winery
Carton Specification		90	80
Runability	90		
Graphic Design	20	10	
Print Quality	80	100	100
Delivery Service	100	40	30
Administrative Service	40	30	30
Technical Service	30		
Sales Contact	60	60	60
Confidentiality	80		
Management Contact	50		

Clearly the small, less automated beer company has a great deal more in common with the wine company than with the large, automated beer company. Further investigation along these lines convinced us that the significant differentiators were size and degree of automation and that they applied across all types of beverage, including soft drinks.

As far as the power tools company was concerned, the group thought of another company producing manufactured products. This company produced industrial fasteners and had a need profile as shown in Table 13.

TABLE 13

	Power Tools Company	Fastener Company
Carton Specification	75	100
Carton Design	80	30
Graphic Design	85	
Print Quality	100	20
Delivery Service	85	90
Administrative Service	35	40
Sales Contact	65	30
Management Contact	15	

These companies clearly belong in different segments with the main differences being related to "graphic design", "print quality" and "carton design". The group attributed these differences to the fact that the power tool company sells to consumers and uses its cases to help sell the product, whereas the fastener company ships its product to another industrial company and is concerned more with the functionality of the case rather than its appearance. Further work on manufacturing companies revealed an additional cause of segmentation related to the variety of product produced. Those with a few standard products or products sold in bulk, e.g. screws, bolts, etc. do not need the same level of carton design or sales contact. The segmentation therefore worked as shown in Table 14 below:

TABLE 14

	Power Tools Company	Fastener Company Specialized	Fastener Company Bulk
Carton Specification	75	100	100
Carton Design	80	30	10
Graphic Design	85		
Print Quality	100	20	20
Delivery Service	85	90	80
Administrative Service	35	40	20
Sales Contact	65	30	10
Management Contact	15		

To test whether or not the segments identified include all those that exist in these types of business, further accounts can be identified and tested against the need profiles of the segments already established. Typically, after all the segments have been identified, there will be some atypical or 'rogue' accounts that do not seem to fit any of the segment need profiles properly.

3.3   Rogue Accounts

The reason for the existence of rogue accounts is generally one of the following:

- the account belongs in more than one segment and its behavior is then either a weighted average of the segments in which it participates, or the account appears to be schizophrenic. These are referred to as "Multiple Segment Accounts".

- the account is either at the leading edge technologically in its segment or has been left behind by the pack and these are referred to as "Segment Leaders" or "Segment Laggards".
- the account behaves differently because of its management style or philosophy. Unless they also fit one of the other classifications, we call these "Losers" or "Winners", depending upon the nature of their differences. For example: a company that is doing something new and different could prove to be the one or the other, or a company that is just out of date and uncompetitive would be a "Loser".

3.4   Multiple Segment Accounts

These accounts are involved in two or more segments. Unless one segment is particularly dominant for historical, profit, or growth reasons, the account will require behavior on the part of its suppliers, who either recognize the segment's need differences or averages its need across all of them. For example, such businesses may serve different markets e.g. consumer and industrial or industrial and government, or may produce a number of products in quite different ways. In any event, from the suppliers' standpoint, it is important to recognize that the customer is involved in each of these different segments and to determine the relative importance of each segment to the customer.

Obviously, as a supplier interested in your clients' welfare, it is desirable to recognize the different segment requirements and discuss these openly in order to ensure the best service to each one. This may involve working with the purchasing department to ensure that you and they are both fully aware of the different needs of the segments that their business serves.

3.5   Segment Leaders and Laggards

Occasionally, a customer is clearly different from the other members of a segment for technological reasons i.e. they are developing or using new technology that makes different demands on their suppliers or alternatively they have been left behind by the rest of the segment. In either case, it is important to recognize this and forecast the future of each account. Behave appropriately, taking into account the probability of their leadership proving successful or their conservatism proving detrimental. For example: when statistical process control (SPC) found its way back to the US from Japan, the companies that first adopted it developed a completely different need profile from those that delayed its implementation. The suppliers that tried to meet their needs would have been rewarded over time as their customers in that segment all adopted SPC.

3.6   Losers

If the account does not fall into any of the above categories, then it is likely to be a business whose management is out of touch with the realities of its business and is demanding behavior appropriate to some other kind of business or to no business at all. This may seem an unlikely occurrence but in fact occurs more frequently than one would believe possible, owing to the real power wielded by Chief Executive Officers, who are not properly chosen in the first place and/or, who are not effectively controlled by their Boards of Directors or vice versa. This situation can also occur when a new CEO, anxious to make an impression, imposes on his or her new organization the policies, standards and behavior patterns typical of the business he or she had come from. This is not to suggest that cross-fertilization is not a good idea, but rather that CEOs and senior management in general should put their egos in their pockets until they understand the business in which they are currently involved and can develop strategies and policies appropriate to it.

As a general rule, "Losers", once identified, should be avoided like the plague because at best they are likely to become a credit risk, and at worst they will go out of business.

So far, we have intentionally avoided the issue of price because it tends to confuse people's perceptions of the other needs. Also, it is very unusual in B2B markets to find two segments which are differentiated solely by their price sensitivity. The segments identified without consideration of price invariably do exist and do not need to be further subdivided into, for example, "price sensitive" and "less price sensitive" segments. However, price is obviously a very important consideration and the next chapter is devoted to measuring price sensitivity.

CHAPTER 4   PRICE SENSITIVITY: THEORY AND PRACTICE

The objective in trying to measure price sensitivity must be to not only determine the relative price sensitivities of different segments, but also to measure the absolute price sensitivity or the price elasticity of demand for a given segment. Where a number of segments use exactly the same product and the actual average transaction prices are known, this information should provide an approximate rank order of the price sensitivities of the segments. This is very useful, but only applies when the same product is used. Also, even in this case, the average prices do not indicate the degree of price sensitivity of each segment, only the rank order.

4.1   Estimation of Price Sensitivity

The approach taken initially to resolve this dilemma was to try to determine what weight the customers in a segment would apply to the need for a low price using the same rating scale as was used in the last chapter for non-price needs. However, the workshop participants at the first experiment could only agree on one thing and that was that price was at least as important as any other need in the segments we were reviewing, which were downstream oil products such as lubricants, aviation fuel, gasoline, etc. In some cases, they could also agree on rank orders of price sensitivity for segments using the same products, but we were unable to develop realistic price weights based solely on their judgement.

The next step was to compare the importance of a low price with everything else in total, or in other words, to add all the weights for the non-price needs and try to develop a weight for the "low price need" relative to this total. The low price weight would thus be based on a ratio of the price need weight to the total of all the other need weights. After further experimentation, it become clear that the importance of price was related to how much variability existed in the actual prices paid in each segment, and in particular, that the more variability there was the less important price was to the buyers.

Also, the idea of the price weight increasing the more like a commodity a market segment is and vice versa also seemed to make sense. In fact, it is very easy to think of segments that would fit at either extreme. For example: large volume gold transactions - a pure commodity market - take place within an extremely narrow range of pricing at any point in time, i.e. very low percent price variability, and the only determinant of whether or not a transaction takes place is price, since the product is by definition, gold of a certain purity. At the other extreme, we find segments for which the value of a product or service lies largely in the eye of the beholder such as artwork, perfume, designer clothes, etc. However, what is also very obvious is that for these extreme cases, the curve is not very useful and if all markets were either commodities or highly personal products, we would not need a curve at all. What does matter is what the curve looks like between these extremes.

There are three ways to determine the shape of the curve. The first and easiest is to try different shapes, calculate the price weight and test the results for accuracy with people who know a particular business very well. This has been done with many groups and in many markets until those groups are comfortable with the end results produced.

The second test is to use the resulting need profiles in combination with performance ratings for the various competitors and see how accurately market shares can be predicted. This process is described in Chapter 8 of this book; for the present, suffice it to say that it has been done very successfully in a wide variety of industries and geographic locations.

The third test, assuming that the second test has been satisfactorily completed, would be to change one competitor's price and see what effect this has in practice in terms of the changes in market shares and how that result compares with the theoretical expectation.

Unfortunately, conditions in the real world do not remain constant long enough in most instances for this test to be completed, since other competitors react to the price change before the full impact of the first price change can be calculated. However, it would certainly be worth tracking some real situations in which this occurred and measuring the timing of reactions and the end result.

Nevertheless, the curve has been used in enough situations using the first two tests for there to be a reasonable confidence level in its utility for practical marketing purposes.

It transpired that the curve is extremely simple and looks like Figure1 below.

FIGURE 1

The figure only shows the curve in the range $x = 0.2$ up to $x = 3.0$ since it is within this range that it has utility. Outside this range, price is either almost irrelevant or the only thing that really matters. In practice, the vast majority of market segments lie within this range.

To be useful in this analysis, the price variability must be "normal". It must exclude short term aberrations resulting from "fire" sales or a dynamic period of price adjustment. Generally, the people involved with the business on a daily basis will know whether or not the current pricing environment is "normal", and if not, then a stable time period from the recent past should be used.

Before giving practical examples of where particular product/market segments fit on the Carey Price Sensitivity Curve, it should be mentioned that individual segments are not constant through time. The needs of a segment can be changed by a variety of factors that impact the economic and business environment, including technology, environmental regulations, competitive forces, "taste", trade agreements, etc. Also, even if a segment does not change fundamentally it can move along the curve at each stage of the business cycle, i.e. expansion, peak, decline, recession.

Most segments move down the curve through the decline to recession and up in recoveries so, for strategic decisions, the relative positions of segments should be reviewed at different stages in the cycle.

4.2   Price Sensitivities in Practice

The examples of price sensitivity shown below are from a variety of industries and countries and for different points in time. They demonstrate the universal applicability of the Carey

Price Sensitivity Curve. The industry examples include newsprint, corrugated cases, industrial lubricating oil, magazine paper (#5 Light Weight Coated - LWC), and to show that it works for consumer products as well, orange juice.

<u>Newsprint</u>

The newsprint example is from the mid 1970s and applies to the Midwest of the US. It identifies three publishing segments, namely Large Urban Dailies (who bought in excess of 25,000 tons per year), Medium Sized Dailies and Weeklies (who bought from 10,000 to 25,000 tons per year) and Small Dailies and Weeklies (who bought less than 10,000 tons per year). The Large Urban Dailies segment is characterized by considerable price sensitivity, a strong requirement for security of supply and the ability to run their printing presses without breaks in the paper (referred to as runability). They are professional in their buying practices, have good technical and legal personnel and use their buying power very effectively. The pricing in each segment was as follows:

- Large Urban Dailies: $220 per ton down to $205 per ton which gives a 7% price variability
- Medium Sized Dailies and Weeklies: $235 per ton down to $212 per ton for a 10% variability
- Small Dailies and Weeklies: $248 per ton down to $215 per ton for a 14% variability

These segments are shown on the Carey Price Sensitivity Curve below (Figure 2).

FIGURE 2

PRICE SENSITIVITIES OF NEWSPRINT SEGMENTS

The price and other performance ratings for the various suppliers yielded very accurate market share expectations which would have been extremely difficult to "fix" since there were twelve separate needs identified, five major suppliers, and a number of smaller ones whose performance was averaged as a group.

Corrugated Cases

This example applies to Australia. The analysis was done in 1993. The corrugated case market contains many different segments and which of these are relevant to a particular business depends upon the economic infrastructure of the area served by a producer. Western Australia has many agricultural and consumer product businesses, but few industrial manufacturing facilities. Five of these segments out of a total of 15 have been chosen for this illustration. They have very different need profiles and wide differences in price sensitivity as well. The segments are as follows:

- Boutique Beverages (wines, specialized beer and other image-conscious beverages): 0.2 price weight ratio
- High Graphic Consumer products: 0.8 price weight ratio
- Large Low Margin Food Processors: 1.1 price weight ratio

- Meat Packers: 0.4 price weight ratio
- Large Agricultural Produce Suppliers: 2.0 price weight ratio

As shown on the Carey Price Sensitivity Curve below (Figure 3), the price sensitivity as measured by the price weight ratio, varies from a low of 0.2 for Boutique Beverages to a high of 2.0 for Large Produce suppliers.

FIGURE 3
PRICE SENSITIVITIES OF CORRUGETD CASE SEGMENTS

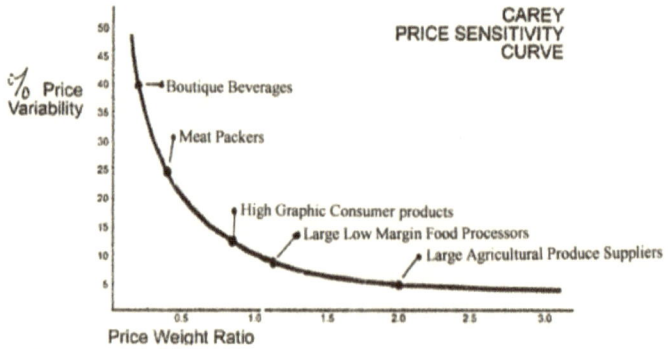

In these segments, the size of the customer's business is obviously of significance and the other differentiating needs are graphic design, print quality, and particularly for meat, product performance. Large produce suppliers use standard cases without significant printing and buy in large volume to be delivered within a short period of time. They are thus very attractive from the production efficiency point of view. The choice of which segments to service thus plays a crucial role in a supplier's manufacturing capability and ultimate profitability.

Industrial Lubricants

The industrial lubricant market referred to here was the Canadian market in 1973, but the segment characteristics for the time were probably universal in the industrialized world. The three market segments identified are the Tender Segment, the Specification Segment and the Performance Segment. The customers in the Tender Segment put their business out to tender for a particular volume of a particular product as defined by its specification over a particular time period. The Specification Segment buys a specified product, but does not go to tender and prefers to buy from whichever suppliers can best meet its needs at a point in time. The Performance Segment buys on the basis of a product's performance in a particular application without reference to a precise specification. These buyers typically have very arduous applications and are looking for whatever works best on their equipment. As a result, there are significant differences in their price sensitivity. The Tender Segment had a price percent variability of only 6%, while the Specification Segment was 15%, and the Performance Segment 25%, as shown below in Figure 4.

FIGURE 4
INDUSTRIAL LUBRICANT PRICE SENSITIVITY

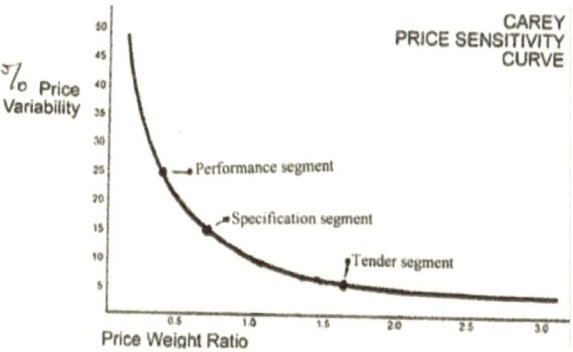

However, since 1973, the industrial oils business has undergone massive change with the development of application specific oils and synthetic lubricants, so that the segments now will be quite different as will the price sensitivities in each segment. This illustrates the importance of revisiting segments and their price sensitivities as the market place and new technological developments occur.

Magazine Paper

The technical term for this paper is #5 Light Weight Coated which is used in all kinds of magazines, a variety of catalogues, coupons, direct mail pieces, programmes, calendars etc. As a result of the wide variety of uses there are also a lot of market segments, including four magazine segments, three catalogue segments, a coupon segment and a commercial printing segment. The price weight ratios varied from a low of 0.6 for printers to a high of 1.5 for the General Consumer Magazines as shown below. Most of the other segments had price weight ratios of less than 1.0, but only the coupon segment at 0.9 is shown because of lack of space.

FIGURE 5
MAGAZINE PAPER PRICE SENSITIVITY

Orange Juice

Orange juice is consumed either for its health benefits primarily or simply for refreshment and there are segments within each of these broad categories. In the case of consumers who bought it primarily for health reasons (in 1993), two segments were identified which we categorized as High Taste and Price Conscious, with high taste meaning that it tastes like fresh orange juice. However, because all consumers were buying for health reasons, even the price conscious buyers were not particularly price sensitive and were primarily concerned with taste and less importantly with ease of use and storage/handling. As a result, the price/weight ratios only varied from 0.3 to 0.4 as shown in Figure 6.

FIGURE 6
FRESH ORANGE JUICE PRICE SENSITIVITY

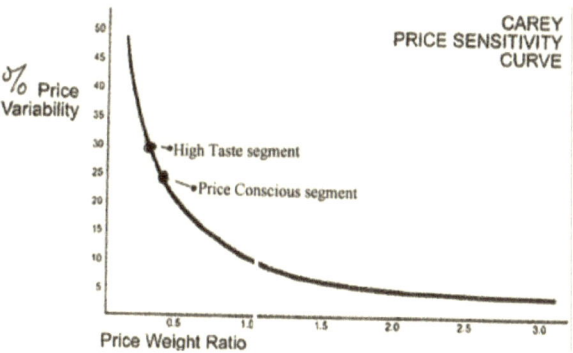

Three other points about price sensitivity are important to remember. First, when a price declines, the buyer expects that the supplier's performance, relative to all the non-price needs, will remain the same. If therefore, the intention is to reduce the level of service to compensate for the lower price, the expected market share gains will only be realized for the time it takes the buyers to become aware of the reduced service levels. After this, the buyers will react very adversely in terms of their performance ratings and market share will decline rapidly.

Second, the greater the role of the purchasing department in the purchase decision, the more price sensitive a customer will become, because getting prices lowered is a large part of the purchasing department's *raison d'être*. Thus, within any segment, the customers with the least purchasing involvement will, over time, probably prove to be the most profitable.

Third, if a company that is the price leader reduces prices, one of two things will happen. Either the other competitors will hold their prices and the price sensitivity of the segment will increase because the variability has been reduced, or more likely, the lower priced competitors will also reduce their prices. Under these circumstances, each company will retain the same share, but will also have lower profitability.

CHAPTER 5   SEGMENT MEASUREMENT AND PRIORITIZATION

Having defined the ways in which a business should be segmented for the analysis to be useful, it is obviously desirable to prioritize the segments in order to generate an appropriate business strategy for growth and profitability. The segmentation process, in effect, divides a business up into a number of different segments defined by product, customer needs, and geography. It might be argued that in addition to the role of geography in determining who the competitors are, there is a further geographical dimension related to distribution costs. However, distribution costs are one of the primary factors in influencing who competes in any area and are therefore taken into account in the identification of competitors.

The market is then shown as a three-dimensional matrix of segments, as shown previously in Diagram 3 and reproduced below. Some of the segments do not exist in practice because a particular product is not used in a market segment or because a market segment does not exist in a particular piece of geography. The first cut in terms of analysis is therefore to exclude the non-existent segments as shown in Diagram 4.

DIAGRAM 4

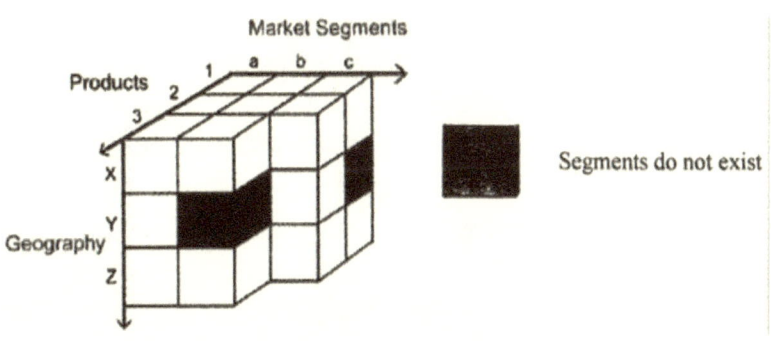

Segments do not exist

In Diagram 4, Segments Y3b and Y1c do not exist. The remaining segments are real in the sense that they currently exist, but any one company may not be involved in them all so that the next "cut" differentiates between segments in which our company is involved, and those in which it is not, as shown in Diagram 5 below. We are not involved in Z2c and Z1c.

DIAGRAM 5

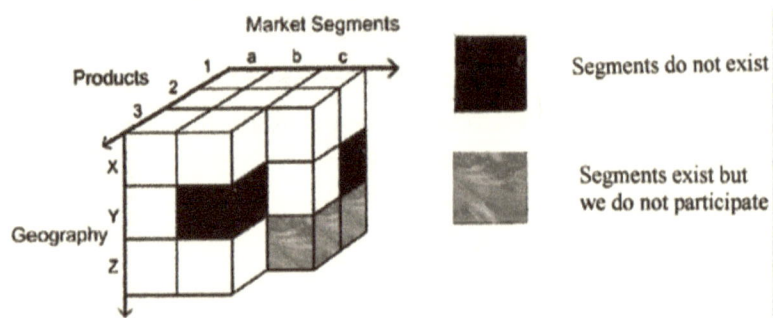

What we have now produced is a three-dimensional representation of the current business and the currently existing strategic issues are:

- On which of the segments should we concentrate our resources?
- Should we exit the remaining segments, or try to "save them" for later development?
- Should we expand into any new segments?

As a first approach to these issues, the segments can be evaluated according to a number of criteria such as segment size, growth, etc. In practice, which criteria are used or considered the most important is dependent upon the nature of the business, but the following usually prove to be significant:

- Segment size: the larger the segment (other things being equal), the easier it is generally to be profitable.

- Segment growth: the faster a segment grows, the more room there is for expansion and hence the easier it is to be profitable over time (see Chapter 10 for a discussion of forecasting issues).
- The competition: the more competitors there are and the stronger they are financially, the harder it is to gain market share, and hence increase volume which impacts profitability.
- Fit: certain segments provide a better fit in terms of each company's capabilities than others, so that a company is more competitive in those segments and can take on more and stronger competitors than in segments with a poorer "fit" (see Chapter 7 Performance Constraints for a discussion of factors affecting "fit").

Using these criteria to prioritize the segments will result in an approximate ranking of their desirability to the business and will provide some guidelines as to which segments should be concentrated on in order to maximize market share and which should be exited. The choice of desirable segments will also typically provide guidance as to how expansion into new segments can most effectively be carried out, since new segments will ideally build upon the product, market or geographic strength of the chosen segments.

At this stage, it may be useful to quickly review what is meant by a niche market. A niche market is simply a market/product/geographic segment, or combination of segments, that are too small or too difficult to service for a large corporation, but are a good fit for a smaller company which can specialise in that segment. One of the advantages of using the segmentation approach is that it clarifies the options available to both large and small companies, and allows the choices to be made in the full knowledge of what is being foregone. This is particularly important for large companies because at some time in the past every segment was small and in many instances were overlooked, until catching up had become extremely difficult or expensive.

The entire procedure is illustrated below using, as the example, a magazine paper manufacturing business. The business produces groundwood gloss printing papers and four segments have been identified in the magazine market as follows:

- General Consumer magazines (GC)
- Medium and high-profile Perfect Bound magazines with classified or other advertising sections (PB)
- Special Interest magazines e.g. Successful Farming, Wood (SI)
- Trade magazines (T)

The geographic segments based on competition are:

- Northeast US
- Midwest US
- Southeast US
- Eastern Canada
- Central Canada

The competition is located predominantly in Eastern Canada, the Midwest and the Southeast US.

We can assign symbols to the degree to which each segment has certain attributes as shown in Table 15 below:

TABLE 15

	+	o	-
Size	big	medium	small
Growth	increasing	stable	decreasing
Competition	weak	normal	strong
Fit	good	indifferent	poor

Finally, each box in the matrix representing a market/geographic segment contains four symbols located as follows:

TABLE 16

Size	Growth
Competition	Fit

When these attributes are assigned to the different segments, we have a matrix that allows us to select the segments with the most profit potential which can then become the target segments for the business.

At this stage, it is perhaps worth reviewing the significance of a segment being targeted or not. The reason for segmenting the market into market segments based on customers' needs was to understand how to satisfy particular customers and thus gain a larger share of their business. The implication of a segment being targeted is therefore that it becomes a component of the focus of the business and how it is operated.

The matrix for this business (Table 17) shows the more attractive segments as light shaded boxes: they are at least neutral if the pluses and minuses are offset against one another. The best segments to target are identified in dark shade. They consist of only two market segments: Special Interest magazines and Perfect Bound magazines. The Perfect Bound segment has four geographic segments.

TABLE 17

	Northeast US	Midwest US	Southeast US	Eastern Canada	Central Canada
SI	o + / - +	o + / - o	- + / - o	- o / o +	- o / o +
T	+ - / - +	+ - / - o	- o / - o	- o / o +	- o / o +
GC	+ - / - +	+ - / - o	- - / - o	- - / o +	- - / o +
PB	o o / o o	o o / o +	- o / - o	- o / + +	- o / + +

If the most desirable segments, in combination, are large enough to absorb production without significant market disruption, then they become the only target segments. However, if they are not large enough, then they become the primary targets in which to maximize share and the other more lightly shaded segments become the secondary targets.

This procedure is rough and ready, since its purpose is to provide guidance as to which segments are most worthy of detailed analysis and the development of specific marketing and sales plans. It is therefore possible that the subsequent detailed evaluation will indicate errors in this initial review. If this in fact occurs, then this prioritization process should obviously be revised appropriately.

CHAPTER 6   SEGMENT ANALYSIS, COMPETITIVE PERFORMANCE AND PERFORMANCE CONSTRAINTS

Prior to the detailed segment analysis, the identity of the segment must be accurately defined in terms of product, geography and market segment. It is vital that the definitions exclude any overlap since that will result in double counting the consumers in the area of overlap.

The first step in the detailed segment analysis is the estimation of its size. In developing this estimate, it is generally easiest to start with an estimate of the total market for the particular product and then break this down geographically and by market segment.

Good numbers are often very difficult to find when the market is broken down by segment so it will probably be necessary to use estimates initially. The estimates can be refined later and additional research may be required. However, the analysis itself will generally help in refining the estimates since it will generate share data which can be used in combination with actual sales to generate an estimated segment size number.

Next, the need profile of the segment must be developed as described in Chapter 3. It is generally a good idea to use the same people who did the initial need profile to do the detailed analysis because they will understand the origins of the needs and their definitions. The third step is then to identify each of the companies active in this segment. Each company or brand will perform in a particular way relative to each need and they are rated accordingly. There is no particular order in which the needs must be addressed except that price is always left until last because the procedure used to estimate price performance is different from the other needs.

6.1   Performance Ratings for Non-price Needs

For each non-price need, each company or brand, starting with one's own, is rated with a score relative to the need weight. Thus, if the need weight is 70 and a company is performing perfectly relative to the need, they will rate 70 with progressively lower numbers for less adequate performances. In all cases, the performance ratings are based on the customer's perception of performance. Generally, the people close to the customers have a good appreciation of how both one's own company and the competition is behaving because the customers will talk about them with very little prodding when the discussion is limited to a particular need, even if they are loathe to rate them on an overall basis, for reasons of confidentiality.

While this process appears to be very subjective, what happens in practice is that each team member argues for their own perception of each company's performance and the sources or reasons for disagreement are clarified. This typically results in a better understanding of the causes for the differences of opinion and a consensus as to what is a reasonable rating for each company and need. The reasons for disagreement are typically related to a lack of concentration on a particular segment. That is, a team member may be thinking of a different geographic area or market segment or even just generalizing about a company's performance. Where significant disagreements continue, the reasons should be noted and placed on a "potential market research project list". Also, as the team members get used to the concept, they become more comfortable, proficient and faster at generating performance ratings.

When this stage is complete, a matrix will have been produced which will look like the one shown in Table 18 below. It is hypothetical and shows an analysis for school exercise books.

The exercise books referred to here are the ones with lined pages used for children to write in which are staple bound, ring bound or perfect bound. The covers come in a variety of colors. The books are ordered by school boards as needed, so that demand is very seasonal with very high volume prior to the start of the school year, low volume once that demand is satisfied and with other blips in demand prior to the start of each term. The other market segment for these books is the retail stationary store segment. The school board market segment is assumed to be 10 million books per year.

TABLE 18

MARKET SIZE: 10 MILLION BOOKS

	Brightwrite	Valuebooks	Schoolbooks
DELIVERY SERVICE	100	70	100	100
LEGIBILITY	80	90/80	80	80
STRENGTH	70	50	70	70
FIXED PRICE	60	60	40	60
ADMINISTRATION	40	30	40	40
PERSONAL CONTACT	80	80	30	40
LOW PRICE	200	100	200	180
TOTAL RATINGS		470	560	570

It is important to note that the ratings should be based on the customer's perception of performance which of course implies some awareness of each company's or brand's product or service. Thus, customers who have no awareness of a particular competitor's performance are simply ignored (they are handled separately through a measure of awareness).

Each of the non-price needs is dealt with in the same way until all of them have a rating for each competitor. Where there are unresolved disagreements, the average value is used as a temporary measure until further information is available.

6.2   Price Performance Ratings

This then leaves only the price ratings to be assigned to each competitor. Because the price need weight refers to the need for a low price, the competitor with the lowest price is normally given the highest rating which is the same as the price need weight. This is the equivalent of full performance for a non-price need weight as shown in Table 18 for Valuebooks.

However, if the lowest price is abnormal because of a "fire sale" or some other kind of short-term aberration, then the low-priced competition is probably exceeding the customer's need. As was shown in Chapter 4 concerning the estimation of the price weight, the distribution of prices within a segment should be used to determine which prices are normal. If a particular price is clearly abnormal, then the extremes of the normal price distribution curve should be used to determine the price ratings, so that the low price is assigned the price need weight and the high price is assigned a rating equal to 50% of the price need weight. The use of 50% rather than any other percentage is based on practical observations in different markets. However, the theoretical foundation for the idea is that in every market there is a price above which nothing will be sold under normal circumstances. Similarly, in assigning ratings to competitors for a service, such as delivery service which is typically very important to buyers, no competitor is normally given a rating of less than half the need weight for delivery service. As with unduly low prices, high prices may find buyers under extreme circumstances, but they are atypical and cannot be used to develop longer term strategies.

How the other competitors are rated depends upon the range and distribution of the competitor's prices. Each competitor is rated on the basis of their average volume weighted prices and assigned the proportionate position between the highest and lowest (legitimate i.e. normal) prices. Thus, if the low price of $20 is equivalent to a rating of 120 and the high price of $40 is equivalent to a rating of 60, then a weighted average price of $30 would rate "90". Each competitor is rated according to the same principle, so that their price performance ratings can be added to their non-price needs performance ratings in order to generate an overall performance rating for each company. The matrix, including price, then looks like Table 19.

TABLE 19

MARKET SEGMENT ANALYSIS
MARKET SIZE: 10 MILLION BOOKS

	WEIGHTS	RATINGS		
		Brightwrite	Valuebooks	Schoolbooks
DELIVERY SERVICE	100	70	100	100
LEGIBILITY	80	90/80	80	80
STRENGTH	70	50	70	70
FIXED PRICE	60	60	40	60
ADMINISTRATION	40	30	40	40
PERSONAL CONTACT	80	80	30	40
LOW PRICE	200	100	200	180
TOTAL RATINGS		470	560	570

The overall performance ratings represent what a company's current performance in the market is (relative to the segment's need profile in the absence of any constraints). In other words, if everyone involved in the purchasing decision in this segment shared the perceptions represented by the ratings, or if the ratings reflect the weighted average in terms of volume purchased, then each competitor's share would be represented by their rating as a percentage of the sum total of all the ratings. To put this in perspective, if each company performed as well as each other, then they would all have the same share. Therefore, to the extent that they do not, the differences in share represented by performance versus the need profile should be reflected in the derived shares.

In the example shown in Diagram 21, the total of the ratings is 1600 and the theoretical market shares would be:

Brightwrite	$470/1600 = 29\%$
Valuebooks	$560/1600 = 35\%$
Schoolbooks	$570/1600 = 36\%$

In reality, there will be many customers who do not know anything about a particular competitor, or have only a partial understanding of their capabilities. This can be the result of insufficient sales coverage geographically or inadequate awareness. Similarly, if the product definition being used encompasses a number of different products and if a competitor produces only half the product range, then this will clearly impact their market share. These diverse causes for the potential share, based on performance ratings, not being reflected, in reality are termed constraints and are dealt with in the next section.

6.3   Performance Constraints and Their Measurement

Constraints cover all the factors that affect a company's real market performance, other than the customer's legitimate perception of current performance. Legitimate in this context means realistic or unbiased.

How any constraint is measured and how it is applied to the performance ratings depends upon the nature of the constraint and how, in reality, it affects a company's performance. Listed below are the common constraints that have so far been identified, although the list may not be all inclusive.

- product line
- distribution
- sales coverage
- customer awareness
- capacity
- brand loyalty or antagonism
- reciprocity

Each of these requires a careful definition and an appropriate measuring technique, to ensure that the final segment analysis reflects reality.

6.3.1 Product Line Constraints

Product line constraints depend directly upon the definition used for "product" in the product/market/geographic segmentation process. For example, if the product is defined as "exercise books", this definition can include both ring bound and perfect bound books. Provided each supplier's market performance is not different for each product, they can be dealt with jointly. However, if the market performance in terms of need satisfaction is different, then they should be dealt with as separate segments. So, assuming they can be combined in the segmentation process, an adjustment may be necessary if some suppliers can produce only one type of product, say, ring bound books. These suppliers are then clearly constrained to the extent that they cannot supply perfect bound books. In this instance, the constraint takes the form of an absolute limitation on their ability to satisfy that part of the segment that wishes to buy perfect bound books and is applied as a percentage to their rating. Thus, if ring bound exercise books comprise 70% of the market and perfect bound the other 30%, then the ring-bound suppliers are constrained to their 70% of the market and the 70% is applied to their rating because their performance rating only applies to that portion of the total segment. This is done by multiplying the company's total rating by 0.7.

Another common product range constraint is the sizes of products within a range, for example bolts or fractional horse power motors. In these cases, it is common for one or more of the suppliers to make only a part of the range. Also, colors or patterns may exclude some suppliers from a piece of the segment. In all instances, it is a matter of comparing each supplier's product offering with the definition of product used in describing the segment from the product standpoint.

6.3.2 Distribution

As with the product line constraint, if a particular supplier can only supply a geographic area smaller than that used to define the segment geography, then their total performance rating is applicable only to the part of the segment they can supply. If the area they can supply represents only 40% of the segment in terms of volume, then a constraint factor of 0.4 would be applied to their total performance rating. Again, the alternative is to redefine the geography that describes the segment, so that it is limited to the geography this supplier actually covers.

6.3.3 Sales

Similarly, if a personal sales or technical service call is necessary to close a sale and a particular supplier covers only 80%

of the segment in terms of sales coverage, then a constraint factor of 0.8 would be applied to the performance rating. However, care should be taken to ensure that this limitation has not already been applied in the form of a distribution constraint since, if it has, the penalty or constraint would be counted twice.

6.3.4   Customer Awareness

Care must be taken in dealing with customer awareness since it can be defined in different ways and how it is defined, determines how to account for its impact on share performance.

First, awareness can mean simply that a part of the segment is not aware of the existence of a particular supplier, or if they know of their existence, they have no perceptions as to their performance. For this part of the segment, such suppliers simply don't exist in terms of the buyer's purchasing behavior.

On the other hand, awareness can also be interpreted as being the same thing as perception. For example, if a supplier has historically performed poorly, then the customer's perception will reflect that. However, if new management changes the level of performance, it will take some time to raise the customer's perceptions to reflect the new reality. This type of awareness is already taken into account in the performance ratings which should reflect <u>current</u> perceptions.

The first type of awareness represents a constraint since those buyers who are aware are assumed to reflect that accurately in their supplier's performance ratings, while for those that are not aware, the supplier does not exist. This therefore has the same impact as a sales constraint and the effect of the constraint is applied as a percentage equivalent to the non-aware part of the segment in terms of volume. Care should be taken to ensure, once again, that there is no double counting. For example: if the reason for the lack of awareness is the absence of sales coverage or distribution capability and this has already been factored in, it should not be included twice.

6.3.5   Production Capacity

If a company is performing particularly well in the market place, it may (through its performance ratings) be entitled to a larger market share than its current capacity. In other words, it is constrained by its capacity. Since its output is limited by its capacity, the additional market share to which it is theoretically entitled will be distributed amongst the other suppliers in the market in proportion to their performance ratings. Clearly, more than one company can find itself in this situation and the procedure to deal with their excess shares is the same in each case.

For some products, increasing capacity can be accomplished very quickly and inexpensively and the situation is unlikely to occur, since typically capacity increases will be triggered when capacity utilization reaches a particular percentage. However, for Capital-Intensive industries, new capacity is very expensive and it may require two or more years to increase capacity; constraints of this type typically occur during the boom of most business cycles and can apply to one or all of the suppliers of particular products.

It is for this reason that many Capital-Intensive industries think that marketing and sales are synonymous. However, the companies that do their marketing well are the last to have to take downtime, when the market turns down, and are the first to reach full capacity in an upswing. Over the course of a ten year cycle, this can easily translate into an operating rate 10 - 20% better than the non-marketers.

6.3.6   Brand Loyalty, Boycotts and Conscientious Objection

Brand loyalty as defined here, refers to a consumer always buying a particular brand. The reason could be habit, a long held belief that it is superior, or the effectiveness of an advertising campaign such as an endorsement. As such, it means that the probability of a consumer buying a particular brand is 1.0 or absolute certainty. Therefore, all the people that buy in this way are not available to the other competing brands. This type of behavior is not unusual in consumer products but is very unusual in B2B markets because professional buyers and specifiers are always looking for the best source of supply. If it does occur, its impact is to exclude the volume affected by brand loyalty from the calculation of market size when estimating the shares based on performance and the other constraints.

Brand loyalty can also work in reverse when a buyer intentionally excludes a brand from their range of choices. Prior to the development of environmental, ethical, religious and special interest activism, negative brand loyalty was not really of consequence. Now however, in both consumer and industrial markets, it can be of consequence and is essentially the reverse of brand loyalty. The reasons are becoming more varied all the time and can include political concerns (such as the boycott of French products that followed the sinking of the Rainbow Warrior), environmental issues, social attitudes, animal rights, genetic modification etc. Again, this behavior is less common in B2B markets but does exist. It is dealt with in calculating shares by excluding the boycotted brand from the list of competitors from which these customers will buy. Thus if 15% of the volume in a segment is controlled by boycotters, then the boycotted brand is competing for the remaining volume only. In other words, their segment size is only 85% of the total segment.

Although brand loyalty is generally of more consequence in consumer marketing than in industrial and B2B marketing, it can be of great importance in cyclical industries in which security of supply is a major consideration. For example: suppliers of pulp (for making paper) may choose to contract their market in a boom by cutting off some customers, in order to maximize short term profits. Those that do this will find that when market conditions weaken, the customers that they cut off will refuse to buy from them, or will exact a penal price for using their product again.

However, because brand loyalty is based on historical preferences or one-off situations, rather than current perceptions of performance, it will tend to be eroded over time unless market performance in satisfying needs is maintained at superior levels.

In industrial markets, in which there is little product differentiation, buyers will attempt to ensure the best value for money, so that brand loyalty can be very short lived and it is very unlikely that a single source will be used. On the other hand, buyers may attempt to maximize value through "partnering" arrangements which provide exclusivity and loyalty to both the seller and the buyer. Also, technical specifications or fit may preclude other suppliers from competing. This has the same market share impact as brand loyalty.

Whatever the cause of the brand or supplier loyalty or antagonism, its overall impact is calculated in the same way. That is, the affected supplier's volume is subtracted from the total segment volume. However, how these volumes are then assigned is, of course, quite different for loyalty and antagonism. Brand loyalty volume accrues directly to the supplier that has earned it and is not available to anyone else, whereas brand antagonism excludes only the targeted suppliers from that volume which is then available to the other suppliers who have not been "blackballed". This in effect creates two market segments: one for "normal" purchasing behavior and one for "blackballed" behavior. The difference between them being the absence, in the latter case, of one or more of the potential suppliers.

6.3.7 Reciprocity

Reciprocity refers to a situation where a supplier and a customer use each other's products and choose to give preferential treatment to each other. For example: one supplies corrugated cases and the other ink. Although reciprocity does not occur as frequently as it used to, it does still happen and has to be handled. Typically, it only happens freely, when the value of the purchase is fairly close to the value of the sale and vice-versa. However, it can be forced in a situation, where one company has great power relative to another. For example: in the province of New Brunswick, if a trucking company wants any of Irving's logging or tanker business, it had better be prepared to buy its diesel fuel from them too! Reciprocity is dealt with in the analysis in the same way as brand loyalty, so that the volume entailed is excluded from the segment in which there is legitimate competition.

6.3.8 Subsidies and Other Forms of Special Treatment

Although not common in North America (apart from Canadian Government contracts), a variety of special treatments such as subsidies or preferential financing are often a part of export marketing. Typically, they have the effect of excluding suppliers who do not have access to the subsidy or other special treatment, and are not therefore part of the competitive market. Their impact is the same as reciprocity and can be dealt with in the same way, by excluding the volume that is subject to special treatment.

It is clear from the volumetric impact that constraints can have, that they are extremely important and are a reflection of the "price of entry" to the market. They represent the marketing investment required in order to participate fully in the segment. Although accountants and bankers do not typically recognize these efforts as investments because they are not "tangible assets", they are nevertheless absolutely necessary for success in the marketplace and are typically reflected in the "good will" assets associated with highly successful businesses. What is also clear is that they require maintenance over time if their value in terms of market share and hence volume and profitability is not to fall into decline.

CHAPTER 7   THEORETICAL VERSUS REAL MARKET SHARE ANALYSIS

The analytical procedure that has been outlined is intended not only to accurately reflect reality, but ultimately to allow market behavior to be simulated, or at the very least to provide effective strategies and marketing and sales plans for a business. We therefore have to ensure that the analysis is representative of reality.

Before embarking on the issue of measurement, that is checking the analysis against reality numerically for market size and shares, it is useful to look at it conceptually to see whether or not it seems to make sense. In order to do this, we can work from a proposition that we know to be logical. As was briefly mentioned in the previous chapter, if there are five competitors in a market and they are exactly the same in terms of performance, brand loyalty, awareness etc., then we would expect them each to have the same market share (namely 20%). To the extent that in real life they don't have 20%, it is because there is something that differentiates them from their competitors, which may be good or bad. If it is good, then they should have more than a 20% share, and if bad, then less than a 20% share. If we can identify specifically what the difference is, then we can start to increase or decrease our estimate of their share in a logical way. The obvious things are what have been referred to as constraints such as awareness, sales coverage and capacity to produce. The less obvious are relative performance in satisfying different needs, but conceptually it all makes sense, so that the issue is then, does the analysis reflect reality?

Initially this type of check must be done for the current market situation, but the same procedures can be used with historical data, if it is available, to ensure that the analysis also reflects the dynamic environment.

7.1   Segment Size Estimates

Unfortunately, the data that is generally available on market size etc. does not correspond to the product/market/geographic segments that have been identified. Available data is typically available for product groups and a geographic area, e.g. a country, and thus is much too aggregated. Some work is therefore required to restate the data in a manner consistent with the segments being analyzed.

There are four possible approaches:

1. Disaggregate the data based on estimates that combine the product and geographic data using one or more proxies for the product such as population or manufacturing output. For example: if the product is gasoline, then fairly accurate estimates can be developed based on population data, so that, if consumption for an area is known and the population is known, the ratio can be applied to a smaller area.
2. Build estimates from the bottom up based on assigning segment codes to each customer and potential customer. Develop estimates of their total purchases based on a relevant variable such as their sales or number of employees.
3. Have the sales force make their own estimates of segment sizes based on their knowledge of their customers and their relative sizes.
4. Use market research.

In practice, the first three in combination usually provide sufficiently accurate numbers for an initial estimate which depending on the confidence level, can be confirmed by collecting additional data over time and by doing market research.

The most common problems are inconsistencies in definitions of products, and less frequently, geography. Typically, the aggregated data is defined more broadly than the product definition in the segment analysis, so the definitions need to be checked for consistency. Industry data usually groups a number of similar products together and identifies them by a generic description. For example, in paper industry statistics, the generic description uncoated fine papers includes a wide variety of different grades of paper, which vary in terms of brightness, smoothness, etc. Also, in the case of geography, the available data may be based on the political map or on the company's operations, neither of which will necessarily conform to the basis on which the segment is defined, which is based on competition.

In practice, it does not really matter if the estimates of size are precisely accurate as long as the segments the business chooses to concentrate on are the right ones. For this purpose, orders of magnitude are generally sufficient. However, the segment analysis itself can also contribute to the estimation, since it automatically generates segment sizes by combining the estimated shares with the company's own sales. Only if there are significant differences between the data estimated externally and the data from the segment analysis would it be worth while doing additional market research, and then only after doing some additional checks on both the external data and the segment analysis.

It is generally more productive therefore to concentrate on making sure the segment analysis is as accurate as possible so that the comparison of segment sizes from external sources and from the segment analysis is meaningful. The sources of errors in the segment analysis are therefore dealt with next.

7.2 Sources of Errors in the Analysis Estimates

The most common sources of errors are the identification and calculation of the constraint factors. The potential problems are as follows:

- A constraint that does exist has been ignored.
- Constraints have been double counted. For example: sales coverage and distribution coverage which apply to the same geographic area.
- The type of calculation used to measure the impact of a constraint is wrong. For example: a distribution constraint applies only to the particular company affected by it, whereas a brand loyalty constraint effectively reduces the size of the competitive part of the segment and thereby affects all the participants.
- An error of judgement or arithmetic has been made in the calculation itself.

Any of these can have a dramatic effect on the relative shares of each competitor and should be carefully checked for errors in the calculations. However, it is also possible that the knowledge base is insufficient to make reasonable estimates, in which case some market research will be required. In the meantime, it is best to use whatever assumptions make the most sense, since as long as they are explicitly identified, it acts as a reminder that better information is needed.

The next most likely causes of error are the calculation of the price weight and the price performance ratings applied to each competitor. The price weight calculation is based on the price differential for a particular segment and there is often a tendency to use the differential for the whole market simply because thinking in segment terms is unfamiliar to most people. The same issue can also be affected by the price ratings calculation, but that is less likely since most companies do not price according to segments anyway. However, the information upon which the ratings are based is necessarily imperfect and there may be errors of judgement that cause problems.

Finally, the ratings given to each company for the non-price performance factors may be wrong. The impact of these is typically much less significant than the other potential errors and can be dealt with more easily also. If a particular performance rating is doubtful, the rating can be given a range from a high to a low and the impact (or sensitivity) of this on the final share can be calculated. If the impact is significant, then some effort must be made to resolve which rating is in fact correct. The easy way to do this is to ask the salespeople or distributors to ask their customers. Normally, when the subject under discussion is a very specific one, customers are only too happy to discuss it with suppliers. Failing that, market research by an independent (and therefore hopefully objective) company may be necessary.

Having reviewed the segment analysis carefully, the market share it generates can be combined with the company's actual sales to the segment in order to produce an estimate of the segment size. This can be compared with the segment size calculated from external data. Generally, they will be found to correspond very well, but if not, then the above procedures should be followed for a second time to identify the problem. If this again fails and the segment is important, then market research is recommended to get a better fix on the size of the segment or the assumptions that have been made.

Even if it proves difficult or impossible to prove the validity of a particular analysis, the work will have had value because it will have forced those involved to explicitly state what all their assumptions are about the market and the competition. At the very least, if it is known that a particular assumption is important, an attempt can be made to verify it, through whatever means are available.

What happens in practice is that as soon as someone becomes comfortable with the techniques used in the analysis, they start to clarify their assumptions automatically and to think in the analytical way that reveals what is going on in the real world.

CHAPTER 8   PERFORMANCE IMPROVEMENT PROGRAMS

The reason for going to all the trouble of segmenting and analyzing the market is of course to decide what needs to be changed (especially what needs to be improved). The analysis will show clearly what is causing a company's market share and/or margins to be less than they could be. However, it should be remembered that nearly everything in the analysis is by necessity an estimate or an assumption and that the cost/benefit estimates will also be approximate. Also, the improvements that are made in performance will take some time to be reflected in the buyer's perceptions. If nothing is done to accelerate these changes in perception by informing the customers ahead of time, then it may take a year or more for the benefits of the improvements to be realized in the form of additional sales.

In order to illustrate how we can use the analysis to estimate the impact of changes in behavior, we will use the hypothetical segment analysis example shown overleaf. Once again, this example uses the school exercise book market.

8.1   The Present Situation

We will assume that our company is the first one shown in Table 20 below, Brightwrite, and that our competitors are Valuebooks and Schoolbooks. Brightwrite supplies both the school board segment and the stationary store segment, whereas Valuebooks and Schoolbooks supply only the school boards. Because it started in the stationary store market, Brightwrite is the only company that produces perfect bound books. Brightwrite only entered the school business about five years ago and has recently persuaded some of the boards to try perfect bound books and to try some new brighter colored covers. Brightwrite has a capacity of 3 million books available for this segment, while Valuebooks and Schoolbooks have capacities of 4 million and 4.5 million respectively.

The relevant customer needs are listed on the left and for the most part are self-explanatory. However, legibility refers to the legibility of hand writing which is achieved, from the product point of view, through a combination of brightness, shade (whiteness), and ink hold out. Strength refers to the strength of the covers and their ability to withstand harsh treatment. Brightwrite's performance relative to each need shows that it is over-performing with respect to legibility, but there is considerable room for improvement in delivery service, strength, administration, and responding to the customer's need for a low price. Because Brightwrite is new to the school business, and because it initially had problems getting used to the different requirements, it has devoted a lot of time to getting to know the school boards' people. It has developed an excellent rapport with them, whereas the competition has been resting on their laurels doing business as usual.

TABLE 20

MARKET SEGMENT ANALYSIS
MARKET SIZE: 10 MILLION BOOKS

	WEIGHTS	RATINGS		
		Brightwrite	Valuebooks	Schoolbooks
DELIVERY SERVICE	100	70	100	100
LEGIBILITY	80	90/80	80	80
STRENGTH	70	50	70	70
FIXED PRICE	60	60	40	60
ADMINISTRATION	40	30	40	40
PERSONAL CONTACT	80	80	30	40
LOW PRICE	200	100	200	180

TOTAL RATINGS	470	560	570
PRODUCT RANGE	1	0.9	0.9
COVERAGE	0.8	1	1
ADJUSTED RATINGS	376	504	513
MARKET SHARES	27	36	37
CAPACITY (,000s)	3,000	4,000	4,500
CAPACITY UTILIZATION	90	90	82

The reasons for the ratings shortfalls for Brightwrite relative to the need weights are as follows:

- Delivery Service: Brightwrite does not have the storage capacity to inventory the volume required at the peak periods and therefore has to ship directly off the machines in September. The result that is it has difficulty putting orders for different quantities and types of book together to try to meet school board orders in time.
- Strength: Brightwrite uses lighter weight cover stock than the other suppliers and its exercise books therefore fall apart more easily.
- Administration is below the needed level because Brightwrite is relatively new to the school board business and has not yet managed to deal with the delivery requirements; the associated complex multi-party invoicing is therefore late as well and is sometimes inaccurate.
- Although our prices ($950 per,000 books) are somewhat higher than our competition we do guarantee a fixed price for the school year and we are the only supplier able to offer perfect bound books which are proving to be more

popular than staple bound books, after their introduction last year.

With respect to Legibility, Brightwrite's paper is brighter and whiter than is currently required by the school boards. Brightwrite also serves the store segment, for which brightness is more important than for the school boards, and it is not worth making two different kinds of book with different paper. However, Brightwrite does not get credit for exceeding the need requirement and its actual effective rating is therefore only 80 rather than 90.

The two competitors are both performing well in all respects except Personal Contact. As has been mentioned, they have become rather complacent and have not matched the efforts of Brightwrite in maintaining excellent relations with the different school boards. As one or two of their sales people have retired, they have not bothered to replace them and their remaining people do not cover the territory as they did previously.

The constraints are coverage which combines sales and distribution, product range which includes both staple bound and ring bound books, and potentially production capacity. As can be seen, the coverage constraint is costing significant market share, but the competition also has product range constraints associated with their inability to supply ring bound books and their limited color range. Everybody has some excess capacity.

8.2   Possible Actions and Their Expected Impact

Having examined the reasons for the performance shortfalls, we can determine what, if anything, we can do about each of the problems and then assess whether any of the available options are worthwhile doing from an economic standpoint. Generally, constraints have the most impact on market share, so we will review them first.

Our coverage constraint results from us being a single plant local producer, within our geographic area, whereas our competitors are national in their coverage with multiple plants. We have not traditionally covered the part of our geographic market segment most distant from our plant because of a combination of meeting delivery dates and high freight costs. However, if we could solve these problems efficiently it might be worthwhile putting in a salesman, who would live in the area. However, if we did that successfully and removed the constraint entirely, we would increase our market share to nearly 30 % and would be dangerously close to exceeding our available capacity. We would therefore have to forego some of the more profitable retail store business or install additional capacity at considerable cost. In view of this, we should examine our other options.

The other options are to improve our service levels in delivery, product strength and administration. Also, we may be able to increase the need weight for legibility, so that we are not wasting that advantage by over performing, although typically attempting to change a segment need weight is more difficult than improving one's own performance. First however, we will review our performance improvement options.

With respect to Delivery Service, our problem is that we have inadequate warehouse space to pre-make product for the busy periods and we have to deliver directly off the machines. This results in both late deliveries and problems in matching mixed orders with the right products. The obvious solutions are to expand the warehouse or to rent warehouse space for the peak periods. Because the additional space is only needed for two months per year, the least expensive solution is to rent space as it is needed close to the manufacturing plant and bring the needed product back to make up orders in our own warehouse. This will keep the external costs low and allow us to meet delivery dates with the correct mix of product. We expect that this will completely resolve our delivery problem and will therefore improve our performance rating to the full need weight of 100. This in turn will improve our total rating to 500 which after adjustment for constraints, will increase our market share by about 1% for a volume increase of 100,000 books. If our price remains unchanged at $950 per thousand books, our revenue will increase by about $95,000. Depending upon our margins and the cost of the external warehousing, we can quickly determine if this is worth doing or not from the short-term profit point of view.

Moving on to the problem of lower cover strength, this issue can quickly and easily be resolved by increasing the weight of the cover stock. However, there will be costs associated with this because the paper will cost more and the weight of the textbook will increase which will result in higher freight costs per thousand books. Again, whether or not this is worth while from the profit point of view can quickly be estimated. The improved strength will increase Brightwrite's rating from 20 to 70 which will improve share by 0.7% and revenue by about $65,000 and again this can be compared with the additional costs of switching to a heavier cover stock. Another option might be to change the type of material to a lighter weight plastic. Again, the relative costs and benefits can be assessed, except that in this instance the issue of disposability and recycling may have to be taken into account and should be reviewed with the school boards before any such action is taken.

The last performance factor we can directly influence is administration. Since our problem is closely related to our current delivery service, if we deal effectively with that problem, we will go a long way towards also improving administration. Perhaps some additional training in the shipping and accounting departments would also help to ensure the proper distribution of delivery notices and invoice copies. We could reasonably expect a small share increase from these improvements worth an additional revenue of about $30,000.

Finally, although we cannot influence the segment need weights through direct action, we can attempt to influence them occasionally. For example, with respect to Legibility, if we can demonstrate justification for the schools to insist on higher brightness paper, we can derive some benefit from the fact that our paper is brighter than our competitors.

The kind of thing that might work would be to investigate any research that may have been done on the relationship between legibility and faster progress by children in reading comprehension and assimilation of facts. If we could show that brighter paper improved childrens' rate of learning, then we would have a case for suggesting that they increase the brightness standard or need weight. This would then generate some value in Brightwrite's superior legibility performance and would contribute more market share worth probably about $30,000.

All the share increases, resulting from performance improvements and the change in the need weight for legibility, amount to roughly 2.8%. This is sufficient to put Brightwrite dangerously close to full capacity and probably warrants a review of the cost of additional capacity, since it will take some time to install the equipment after the decision is made. Part of that review would be the potential for increased share if the sales and distribution constraints were removed. The potential would be an increased share of nearly 5%, which translates into revenue of $475,000 (500,000 exercise books at current prices).

When all of these changes have been enacted, the segment analysis will look like Table 21 below.

TABLE 21

MARKET SEGMENT ANALYSIS
MARKET SIZE: 10 MILLION BOOKS

	WEIGHTS	RATINGS		
		Brightwrite	Valuebooks	Schoolbooks
DELIVERY SERVICE	100	100	100	100
LEGIBILITY	90	90	80	80
STRENGTH	70	70	70	70
FIXED PRICE	60	60	40	60
ADMINISTRATION	40	40	40	40
PERSONAL CONTACT	80	80	30	40
LOW PRICE	200	100	200	180
TOTAL RATINGS		540	560	570
PRODUCT RANGE		1	0.9	0.9
COVERAGE		0.8	1	1
ADJUSTED RATINGS		432	504	513	1449
MARKET SHARES		29.8	36	37
CAPACITY (,000S)		3,000	4,000	4,500
CAPACITY UTILIZATION		99.3	90	82

8.3   Evaluating Changes In Price

So far we have assumed that we would keep our price constant and try to increase share by improving performance in the non-price needs. There are two reasons for this. First, if we fix the non-price needs, the competition is going to take quite a while to realize what has happened because the changes are relatively subtle, and apart from the legibility issue, are unlikely to attract a lot of comment. Second, price reductions are invariably perceived for what they are which is an attempt to buy market share. Naturally, customers will be only too happy to pass this information on to competitors in order to get similar reductions from them. The usual net result of this is that everyone ends up with the same share, but at much lower prices because what normally ensues is a price war. This strategy can work but only under very special circumstances. Specifically, the company initiating the price war must have the lowest costs in the business and a war chest to see it through to its logical conclusion which is to put one or more competitors out of business. Unfortunately, what happens more frequently is that the target companies are bought by someone else with deeper pockets. It then takes them some time to realize that they are going to find it very difficult to make any profit, so that the poor prices continue for much longer than anticipated. In the vast majority of cases, price reductions are only effective in "fire sale" situations on off-grade material where the reduction can be justified by the poor quality and the absence of normal service.

Another option is to increase prices which would result in a lower price performance rating and hence a reduction in market share and volume, and hence result in higher production costs. However, if everybody is operating at or close to full capacity then the competition would be unable to increase production, at least in the short run, and would probably follow suit, so that profitability would increase without any attendant cost increases.

In summary, any action will result in changes in market performance and hence in market share which in turn changes production volume. The segment analysis allows us to estimate what these changes will be and the next chapter goes into more detail concerning the calculation of costs and benefits.

It should now be apparent that what has been created is a way to simulate market behavior, which allows us to estimate the consequences in financial terms for any slate of actions that may be taken either by our own company or by any competitor.

CHAPTER 9   COSTS VERSUS BENEFITS &
         SEGMENT AGGREGATION

9.1   Calculation of Costs Versus Benefits

The previous chapter introduced the measurement of benefits resulting from performance improvement, need weight changes and constraint removal. This chapter deals in more detail with the calculation of financial benefits resulting from performance improvement and constraint removal and introduces the calculation of costs in a more detailed and all-inclusive way. This will facilitate segment aggregation and the estimation of total costs and benefits for any slate of actions.

The advantage of analyzing the individual segments in some detail is that the reasons for a performance shortfall have already been built into the performance numbers by the people doing the ratings, so that they know precisely what it is that needs to be improved. This precision in problem identification usually leads directly to a number of possible ways of solving the problem, each of which may be a total or a partial solution and will have a set of costs associated with it. If the problem seems intractable, there are a number of very effective creative problem solving methodologies that will typically result in a number of potential solutions for evaluation.

Before examining the calculation of cost/benefits from performance improvement, it is probably useful to take a brief diversion to review the role of accounting practices in these calculations. The costs fall into one of four categories, two of which (variable costs and fixed production costs) are directly related to the manufacture of the product or the provision of a service, and the others are overhead and R&D. Under normal circumstances, R&D expenditures do not come into play and are dealt with separately in a later chapter.

Since almost any change in behavior will have an impact on the volume produced, the fixed and variable costs of production must be known in order to calculate the financial impact of a particular volume change. Unless the facility is running close to full production, almost any additional volume will have a beneficial cost impact in addition to what it does on the revenue side, since the fixed costs are spread over a larger volume. Unless there is a change to the nature of the product, variable costs will track volume increases. However, while this is perfectly straight forward in theory, in practice the allocation of costs, as fixed or variable, is a whole study in its own right and different procedures are used in different companies, depending upon the background and interests of the person in charge. It is therefore incumbent upon the marketing professional to understand how costs are allocated in practice, in order to correctly calculate the cost impact of a change in volume which may not be the same as the accounting allocation of costs. What we have to be concerned with is reality and not accounting form.

The vast majority of other costs associated with doing things differently in the marketing and sales arena are considered as simply overhead, that is, they are expensed annually against revenue and are treated in the same way as purely administrative expenses. In this respect, even though they may be identified separately, and may be deducted as marketing and sales expenses before the rest of administrative overhead, they have the same bottom line impact as accounting, legal, human resources etc. However, there is one significant difference between marketing expenses and other administrative expenses, which is that marketing can have a major longer term impact. This is because brand loyalty is an asset in its own right, even though it is not accounted for until a business is sold, at which point it appears as "good will". As was discussed in Chapter 6, brand loyalty can be increased through judicious marketing management or destroyed through incompetence.

Returning to the calculation of performance cost/benefits, we can calculate the volume cost effect of an action if we know the fixed and variable costs of production. The marketing costs can typically be estimated quite accurately, provided the actions to be taken are clearly identified. For example: referring back to the exercise book case, if we decide to improve our delivery service through increasing our warehouse capacity, we will have the following costs:

- Construction and equipment costs which can be depreciated over the expected life of the assets
- Additional labor which constitutes a marketing expense, but will probably only be required on a seasonal basis
- The cost of holding the additional inventory which can be represented by the average value of additional inventory for the period for which it is held, multiplied by the firm's cost of capital
- The cost of any additional planned promotional tools

Apart from the promotional tools, which are discretionary, all the other actions must be taken to resolve the problem and the degree to which performance will be improved must be decided upon. For example: it may be possible to improve performance to 95% of the need weight for a particular amount of money, but will cost a further 50% to ensure 100% performance. Under these circumstances, it will be more profitable to settle for 95% performance.

All the proposed cost items can then be compared with the additional revenues generated by the improved performance, bearing in mind that there will be a lag between the cost impact and the revenue impact, since it will take time for the improved performance to be reflected in different purchasing behavior. The additional revenue will come from additional volume, and at current margins, will result in additional gross profit. From this must be deducted the above mentioned incremental costs which will result in either an incremental net profit or a net loss for this segment. If the benefit is marginal, then it is a good idea to calculate the costs and revenue over a five year period. The performance analysis calculates market shares which, assuming there is growth, must be applied to the higher future segment size numbers. However, the decision to proceed or not must wait until the impact of the change in performance on other segments is assessed, also because something that cannot be justified based on one segment may have significant benefits in other segments. The calculations of various cost/benefits are shown for a the single school book segment, using hypothetical numbers, in Table 22 below.

TABLE 22

	Marketing costs	Fixed production costs	Variable production costs per 1,000 books
Need weights			
Legibility			
Promotional Literature: summarize the research re. legibility	$1,500		
Direct mail the literature	$180		
Performance ratings			
Delivery			
Warehouse space addition: capital cost of $120,000 amortized over ten years	$12,000		
Inventory: additional inventory valued at $300,000. Cost of capital 5%	$15,000		
Order response time			

Customer Service: add one person	$45,000		
Training: supervisor's bonus	$2,000		
Strength			
Product Upgrade: heavier cover stock @ $10 per 1,000 books			$10
Constraints			
Distribution			
Use external carriers @ $15 per 1,000 books	$10,5000		
Sales Coverage			
Additional travel and communications charges	$10,000		
Capacity			
Facility Upgrade		$60,000	($6)
Total for segment	$96,180	$60,000	$4

The cost numbers have to be related to the resultant change in performance, since it may require a combination of actions to achieve the desired performance change or it may be possible to take a number of separate actions each of which has an independent impact on performance. As a result, they are initially expressed as costs per unit of performance improvement and then aggregated for the segment .

Because the way in which the cost/benefit numbers are calculated is consistent, these calculations can, in practice, be automatically done on a computer, once the appropriate cost assumptions, or estimates, for the actions are made. Similarly, if capacity is increased, the cost/benefit ratio can be determined by comparing the various cost changes, before and after the increase in capacity, with the revenue and profit numbers before and after. In most cases, increasing capacity would not be contemplated unless it was expected that there would be immediate incremental volume to utilize the new capacity, so that the additional capacity would be removing an existing market constraint. However, whether or not it would make economic sense to proceed with a capacity addition will depend once again, in part, upon future growth.

Also, when capacity is increased, there are typically productivity improvements that also accrue to the manufacturer because the capacity increase will remove a bottleneck. In the case of the exercise books, if the capacity constraint is the printing capability, then removing it will allow the binding equipment to run at higher capacity also. As a result, the fixed costs of the binding equipment are spread over the additional volume, resulting in lower total costs per unit and higher gross margins. Other constraints such as sales, distribution and awareness can be dealt with in very similar ways. The removal of a constraint results in increased market segment share and hence additional revenue at the same margins as previously and this provides the benefit number. This must then be compared to the costs associated with removing the constraint. The removal of constraints typically requires a continued annual expenditure that becomes part of the overhead. The exception to this is improving awareness which obviously requires much more up front expenditure and can be cut back as awareness increases.

Table 23 below shows the total expected result from a slate of actions in the school board exercise book segment. Because we are looking at this segment in isolation so far, the option of expanding capacity is less attractive than running at close to full capacity and increasing price, but the positive impact of all the other actions is clearly demonstrated.

TABLE 23

	Base case	Simulation	Change $	Change %
Revenue	3,136,500	4,180,000	1,043.000	33.26
Variable production Costs	1,660,500	1,997,600	337,100	20.30
Marketing costs		91,180	91,180	
Segment contribution	1,476,000	2,091,220	615,220	41.68
Volume(,000 books)	3,690	4,400	710	19.24
Price per 1,000 books	850	950	100	11.76
Capacity Utilization %	92.25	95.65	3.4	3.68

The output from this effort will be a list of possible action plans with their associated incremental costs and benefits for whichever segment was considered the highest priority. In the case of our simplistic exercise book example, there are only two segments, so it is relatively simple to review possible performance improvement options for both segments and then determine what synergies exist between the two. For example: if increasing capacity results in lower costs, these benefits will automatically be felt in the other segment because both segments use the same product. In most real businesses, the aggregation of the changes in costs and benefits is quite complex and a computer is needed to do the aggregation across all the different segments.

However, it is still necessary for human judgement to be used to identify some of the possible synergies and to ensure they are properly accounted for in the overall impact of the action plans. The next section reviews many of these synergies and discusses the factors that generally have the greatest impact.

9.2   Segment Aggregation

The aggregation of costs and benefits across all the segments, while quite demanding in terms of time and management input, is also very rewarding because nearly everything that is done to improve performance in one segment generally also has some benefits in other segments. For example: if product quality is improved, it will often have an impact nearly everywhere, as will improvements in delivery capability, administrative efficiency, technical service etc. The initial task is to review the impact of performance improvements designed for one segment on all the other segments. Typically, this will involve estimating the improvement in performance ratings and calculating the impact of the higher performance ratings or constraint elimination on market share and hence on volume.

However. great care must be taken to ensure that the definition of each affected need is the same in each segment. For example: delivery capability may mean JIT in one segment and "at the same time each week" in another. Obviously, if the improvement is to ensure "at the same time each week", it will not help in JIT segments. Also, in segments that do not need the improved performance, there will be no increase in market share, unless some other actions are taken to increase the need weight, as was shown in Chapter 9 with respect to changing the need weight for exercise book product quality by creating a new brightness standard.

With respect to price adjustments, these too will have an impact outside the segment for which they are primarily intended, unless it is possible to isolate a particular segment by changing the product in some way, or branding it differently. This becomes extremely important from the point of view of competitive reactions. Typically, a competitor will have no way of knowing that a price change is intended only for a particular segment and a price reduction intended for only one segment may end up destroying prices in the market in general, that is, across all the segments. It is therefore vital, if price changes are contemplated, that they be isolated in the segment in which they are intended to have an impact. Any re-branding or re-packaging of the product to differentiate it from the original must be synchronized with changing the price. Also, the costs of the packaging or brand changes must obviously be included in calculating the profit impact of the price change.

Constraint elimination may also have an impact outside the segment for which it was primarily intended. For example: if geographic sales coverage is improved by appointing a sales rep to an area not currently serviced, then it would be foolish to limit the rep's activities to only one segment. Similarly, distribution coverage, product range additions and many ways of improving awareness will affect more than the initially targeted segment. When the aggregation across all segments is complete, the resultant action plans and total cost benefit numbers provide the sales forecasts, pricing plans, capital and departmental budgets for all the areas affected by new or different behavior.

CHAPTER 10   SIMULATION TECHNIQUES

Thus far, we have only used the market analysis as a planning tool in which we know what we want to do and can calculate the approximate cost and benefits of doing it. However, the real power of the methodology lies in its ability to simulate the impact of a variety of different actions as well as what we expect the competitive reactions to be over time. For example: using the textbook case again, we assumed that the best way to solve the delivery problem was to rent outside warehouse space because the need was seasonal. However, since the business also serves the stationery store market, when we aggregate the segment analysis, it may be better to build additional warehouse space, if we also intend to expand the stationary store business through geographic expansion. The cost and benefits of doing this can be calculated and compared to the renting space option.

The types of events and actions that can be simulated include the following:

- Changes in our company's performance relative to needs (including quality and all aspects of service and delivery)
- Different pricing options
- Removal of constraints
- Changes in competitive behavior
- The effect of market growth and capacity changes
- The sensitivity of financial results to all the relevant variables

Clearly, for any but the simplest business, it is preferable to use a computerized model that incorporates all the relevant data. Once the key segmentation and market analysis work has been done and loaded in the model, doing any kind of simulation is very straightforward.

10.1   Simulating Performance Improvement

There is a myriad of marketing tools that would typically be used to improve performance and the art of marketing lies in deciding which to use to address each problem. These are generally categorized in consumer product marketing texts as the four Ps: Product, Packaging, Price, and Promotion, but a broader scope and a more detailed list is needed for B2B marketing. Any terminology can be used provided that everyone involved has the same understanding of each term's meaning. A check list of useful terms is provided in Appendix A.

Because the simulation works with both financial data and market data, it is vital that expenditures associated with various possible actions are properly identified. The simulation model works on the basis of incremental changes in cost and revenues relative to the current situation. Therefore, if an expenditure is a straightforward marketing expenditure such as adding a salesman, it would be added to the marketing overhead and the majority of marketing expenditures will fall into this category. However, if the action will affect production or packaging then its impact on production costs must be taken into account since the entire volume of production of the product will be affected. Thus, if a product is upgraded by a change in its composition, its variable cost will be changed, and if there is also an addition of new equipment, there will be changes in both variable and fixed costs. The simulation therefore differentiates between actions that impact production costs and those that do not.

One of the reasons the simulation approach outlined here is very effective is because everything that may require action is tightly and explicitly defined in the initial analysis. For example: if a poor performance rating for product quality has been given, then the reasons for that rating are also clearly stated. There may of course be a number of quality related issues contributing to a low rating, and if so, then each will have been clearly stated and the contribution of each element to the performance rating will have been estimated as part of the analysis. Obviously, the more precise the definition of the problem is, the easier it will be to develop appropriate remedies. While simulation does not produce the ideas for remedial action, it is very helpful in ensuring that the problem is properly defined and allows a fast analysis of the cost relative to the expected benefit for any slate of actions.

The simulation also allows the marketing personnel to estimate what the benefits will be of taking action to improve performance. In the vast majority of businesses, this will be a new experience because marketing people are typically in the position of wanting various things to be improved, but are unable to estimate what the benefits will be. As a result, they are usually on the defensive, since in most cases, improving performance costs money. They are always in the position of griping about things to the production, warehouse, logistics or administrative personnel, and as a result, a great deal of energy is wasted in arguing about the pros and cons of taking action.

For example, if we have a shortfall in quality of 30 points relative to the need weight for "quality" of a paper product and this shortfall is due partly to inconsistency and partly to shade, we can attribute the shortfall in the most realistic way, say 20 points for inconsistency and 10 points for shade. We then believe that fixing the inconsistency will earn us 20 points of improvement while fixing the shade will earn us 10 points. However, anything to do with quality automatically involves the production department. They will generally say that it is a lot more difficult to fix a consistency problem than it is a shade problem. This is because the former is typically the result of a combination of things including raw material consistency and the reliability of the paper machine, whereas shade can usually be adjusted by changing the pigment mix in the paper furnish.

However, if there are consistency problems because of, say, the paper machine, then they are likely to affect every product made on that machine and every segment that uses each product. Thus, if consistency is indeed a problem, then the marketing department can use the simulation to make a reasonable estimate of what the reward for fixing the problem will be and, instead of just complaining about consistency they can, jointly with the production department, make the case for fixing the problem. Thus, it may well be a better option from a single segment cost/benefit point of view to change the shade, but from a broader perspective it may be better to fix the consistency problem. At the least, raising the issue will result in everyone getting a better understanding of the consistency problem and its causes and an idea of the benefits from fixing it.

Similarly, if there is a problem with delivery service, the marketing people can, jointly with the logistics people, try to find effective solutions with the knowledge that they can justify some level of expenditure in terms of increased market share, and hence revenue.

For every other performance issue, because the reason for a shortfall has been identified, the possible ways of solving the problem can generally be also imagined and the benefits can be calculated across all the segments affected.

Occasionally, developing effective and economic solutions to solving performance problems proves difficult. Under these circumstances, it may be useful to employ one of the many creative problem-solving processes in order to generate ideas which can be refined into workable solutions. When they have been refined to everyone's satisfaction, their financial impact can be simulated using the model.

10.2   Different Pricing Options

The problem with simulating different pricing options does not lie in calculating the impact, but in predicting what the competitive response will be. As has been mentioned, price reductions may start a price war and have no effect on market share. Similarly, a price increase in a growing market may be followed by the competition, so that again there is no change in shares. The trick is thus in being able to predict the competition's reaction if a price change is made openly. This typically requires a very good understanding of the competition's management, marketing strategy, and financial circumstances, and to the extent that this understanding is lacking, justifies the time and effort involved in getting this information.

Price increases are much less critical than decreases, since they will normally only be tried when a product is close to full capacity, and if the competition does not follow suit, the price increase can be rescinded. However, when announced prices are decreased, other than for short term clearance or loss leader sales, the likelihood is that the competition will follow suit in order to retain market share and everyone will keep their current shares, but at lower prices. This strategy is therefore only appropriate when the intention is to put a competitor out of business, or to drive down their profitability, so that they can be acquired inexpensively. This obviously requires that there be a weak competitor in the sense that they cannot survive a price war and that the company initiating the war has a sufficient war chest to survive and to buy the target company if that is the intention. To be effective, a price war should be over quickly or the costs will out-way the ultimate benefit.

The simulation model is very useful in allowing the financial impact of a price war to be calculated based on whatever assumptions or options need to be evaluated. Thus, the amount of a decrease, the length of time it will be in place, and the expected competitive reactions, can all be factored in and the impact on the target competitor can also be calculated. It should also be recognized that other competitors may be interested in an acquisition, so that if the intention is to make a cheap acquisition, this may be thwarted. The very real possibility therefore often exists that the entire exercise will prove to have been in vain and everyone will simply end up a lot poorer.

However, there are a variety of other ways of legally changing prices in order to increase market share that do not make the change as public, although there is always the risk that customers will play one supplier off against another. These include offering volume discounts or rebates, discounts based on the customer buying a particular mix of products, reciprocity deals or barter trading, or as has already been mentioned, re-branding a product (generally difficult in B2B markets in which brand names and packaging are not typically important). Whatever the price change proposed, the difficulty will always be in predicting whether or not the customer(s) will maintain confidentiality (if appropriate), and if not, how the competition will react. The simulation is by comparison straightforward and the expected share increase can readily be simulated for whatever action is proposed. The simulation procedure, where the action is intended to be limited to a few customers, is to apply the same principles as are used when calculating the impact of product range constraints. Thus, if volume discounts are made available to a few accounts, then they are separated from the rest of the segment, and in effect, become a segment of their own in which the pricing and competition are different.

10.3   Removal of Constraints

Constraint removal typically has the greatest impact on segment share, but also tends to be expensive since it is the constraints that represent barriers to entry. Simulation will quickly show the benefits to be derived from constraint removal, but developing the most efficient way to accomplish the task is much more difficult unless the constraint is related to product range, in which case the action required to remove the constraint is self-defining.

However, if the constraint is distribution coverage or awareness, there are a multiplicity of ways to change these situations and each will have associated costs and estimated benefits. Also, the best plan may involve a combination of three or four different actions in order to accomplish the desired change. The simulation model will calculate the cost/benefit result for the proposed slate of actions and estimated benefits.

Generally, estimating costs is much easier than estimating benefits, but because the problem has been specifically identified relative to a segment, it is in practice not too difficult to estimate the impact that a particular course of action will have. If a particular program will be expensive and the benefit is difficult to estimate, then it will make sense to do a small trial to evaluate the response. This is particularly true for constraints like awareness in which there are a wide variety of possible tools available which will probably differ significantly in their costs and effectiveness.

As far as the other possible constraints are concerned, capacity is straightforward from a simulation standpoint, although it requires estimates of the capital cost and the impact on variable costs. Also, the appropriate time frame for when the additional capacity will come on stream must be estimated, as well as the expected volume of sales at that time which will include the volume impact of performance improvements, constraint elimination, and segment growth.

As far as reciprocity is concerned, there is not normally much one can do about other people's reciprocal arrangements, but it may be possible to arrange reciprocal arrangements of one's own by way of retaliation. Also, competitive brand loyalty can only be addressed through a combination of improved performance over time and increasing awareness of that performance. However, whether or not antagonism expressed through boycotts can be addressed effectively, depends upon the cause of the antagonism and whether it is the result of a real situation or simply perception. For example: a real situation might be that the company is polluting a river and doing nothing to fix the problem. On the other hand, if the company is being accused of something for which it is not responsible (for example, the above mentioned pollution actually comes from someone else's plant upstream), then action can be taken to correct this perception and get the boycott removed.

With all constraint related issues, the impact of the removal of the constraint is to remove the penalty that the constraint imposed in the first place which will result in increased share and volume. This can once again be simulated before taking any action to ensure that the result is financially beneficial.

10.4   Changes in Competitive Behavior

The most radical changes are of course when a competitor goes out of business and when a new competitor enters the market. If a competitor goes out of business and the production capacity is scrapped, then that competitor's share of the business becomes available to the remaining companies, and other things being equal, will be divided up in proportion to their existing shares. However, if another company buys the manufacturing equipment, then that effectively increases that company's capacity accordingly and the company will either have to do something differently to fill it, or wait until the market grows sufficiently to absorb it. The expected behavior can be readily simulated and contingency plans can be prepared for this eventuality.

The addition of a new competitor is more difficult to simulate unless the likely behavior of that competitor is known from other segments. If nothing is known, then three separate simulations should be run. The first would assume that the new competitor's performance is as good as the best of the existing competitors, the second should use the average performance of the other competitors, and the third should use the worst performing competitors' ratings etc. This then provides a range within which the impact of the additional supplier will lie and allows alternative responses to be evaluated using the simulation model. These alternative responses become contingency plans for this possible eventuality. However, these simulations and the necessary responses can be done quite quickly, so that unless there is a reasonable likelihood of this happening, there are probably better things to be concerned about.

Other changes in competitive behavior are generally very easily simulated by adjusting the competitor's performance or constraint ratings to reflect future expectations. If for example, it is learned from a customer that a competitor will be filling out their product range in the near future, the product range constraint can be adjusted accordingly and the impact on share and profitability estimated. This may or may not require adjustments in our own marketing plan. Similarly, if it is learned that a new sales representative has been appointed to cover a territory from which that company was previously absent, the constraint adjustment will be reflected in the overall rating and hence share and profitability. Other changes are handled in a similar way and responses can be planned to suit the new situation.

10.5   Simulating the Effect of Market Growth and Capacity

Market growth is very easily simulated by increasing everyone's volume at the expected rate of growth and it is also crucial that this be done whenever the forecast rate of growth changes in order to allow sufficient time to plan and build additional capacity. The number of years into the future that should be forecast depends upon the lag between the decision to increase capacity and the capacity coming on stream. Initially, this calculation is done on the basis of other factors remaining unchanged. However, what happens frequently in capital-intensive industries is that nobody thinks about increasing capacity until they are running full. In order not to be left behind in the race to expand, everyone then increases capacity at the same time, resulting in massive gluts of over capacity which since Murphy's Law (whatever can go wrong will go wrong) always seems to apply, invariably coincides with an economic downturn. The result is years of poor earnings performance unless high cost capacity is shut down or converted to a different product.

If the growth rate is forecast effectively and often, then the best performing company, that is the one with the highest operating rates, ought to be thinking about expansion well ahead of everyone else with the others following at the appropriate time. In this way, there would be an orderly increase in capacity, so that there is neither a glut nor a shortage, unless the economy takes a sudden downturn. Even then, the impact on the industry would be much less severe than if everyone runs with the herd.

The comments about market growth suggest that everyone should try to forecast, and it is vital that the forecasts bear some resemblance to reality. Unfortunately, in many cases this assumption is false, and capacity is added on the basis that it will be lower cost than existing capacity and so will provide an economic return. This is particularly true of capacity in third world countries where businesses are often built with little regard to the environmental impact they will have, and the low cost of labor combined with poor environmental management can result in very low production costs. While nobody should begrudge developing countries the opportunity to grow and increase their standard of living, it is unfortunate if this is done at the expense of future generations through the destruction of the environment. Nearly all industries are now international in their scope and the forecasts must be made on an international basis.

Having said this, there are also examples of new technologies with very high natural growth rates that are concentrated in the developed countries which nevertheless manage to build massive over capacity in a race for industry leadership. The broadband over capacity and the meltdown in stocks in the communications industry was a good example of the futility of building unneeded capacity which could easily have been avoided if the companies involved had done their homework properly.

The simulation model will demonstrate clearly the financial futility of pursuing these kinds of capacity increases which far outstrip any conceivable growth in demand. Demand forecasting is not a topic peculiar to this book and there are an abundance of good forecasting techniques available and product forecasting these days with ready access to economic and technology adoption forecasts, need not be expensive.

10.6   Sensitivity Analysis

One of the most obvious advantages of simulation modeling is that it allows the sensitivity of the bottom line to changes in any variable, to be calculated. Financial models provide this ability for variables like interest rates, margins, variable costs etc., but not for what causes these variables to change, nor for what their impact may be on other variables. Simulation allows the strategist and marketer to change all the real world root causes of the revenue stream and costs in order to ensure that there is always an awareness of what is happening to the factors that have the greatest impact on the business.

To illustrate the difference between the power of a financial model versus simulation, consider how each deals with a change in price for a particular product. The financial model will change the price without changing the volume, or will use an algorithm for price sensitivity to adjust the volume. The simulation model on the other hand, forces the user to make some assumptions about competitive behavior in response to the price change, and develops the revenue sensitivity based on the change in market shares that results from the price adjustments. While this will not appeal particularly to an accountant who wants a number to put in a budget, it should be of immense interest to the operating management, who have to make the decisions about price changes. In other words, simulation is an operating management tool that helps managers make the correct decisions and explain those decisions to everyone involved.

The effect of this is of course to build a culture of personal involvement, so that everyone has the same understanding of why things are done and the opportunity to have input in the decisions that directly affect them.

For those who are used to using simulations and wish to harness all their benefits, Monte Carlo simulations can be used in conjunction with the basic business simulation. Monte Carlo simulations allow the user to assign probability distributions to the variables of most interest and to develop a most likely outcome as well as providing the range of probabilities for other outcomes. The effect of this is to make perfectly clear which events are likely to have the greatest impact on results, and therefore provide guidance as to the types of contingency plans needed.

CHAPTER 11   BUSINESS PLAN DEVELOPMENT

What has been described and explained thus far is a methodology to segment and analyze markets in detail, prioritize them for the purpose of devoting time to the most important segments, and to allow behavior to be simulated so that its effect on the bottom line can be estimated. This can then lead to the development of appropriate action plans to maximize profitability in the chosen segments. However, so far we have dealt with each segment as though it is a "mini-business" on its own and tried to maximize each segment's contribution to the overall effort. Also, to the extent that actions in one segment impact other segments, this has been taken into account and their impact can be estimated for the business as a whole. We have therefore developed a tool that allows us to determine how to maximize the potential from the internal growth of the whole of the existing business. This we can call Strategy #1, that is, "maximize profitability from internal growth" and if we execute these plans, we will have maximized our share of each of the segments that are attractive, working on a sliding scale of attractiveness down to those segments that are least attractive. In most businesses, this will mean that for some products they will be operating at full capacity and will require that sales to the least attractive segments be constrained. In essence, we have developed a segment hierarchy for all the market/product/geographic segments in which the company operates.

To illustrate how this works in practice, there follows an example based upon a corrugated case business which serves five market segments and which for the sake of simplicity, we will assume operates within a limited piece of geography. The company has sufficient capacity to satisfy 28% of the market. Table 24 shows in descending order of attractiveness, the market segments available and their size, and based on the market analysis, simulations and the eventual marketing plan, the segment shares that we expect to achieve in each segment. These shares are then expressed in volume terms until the cumulative total equals full capacity operation.

TABLE 24

Segment	Priority	Volume	Target Share	Volume	Cumulative Volume	Cumulative % Capacity
Boutique Beverages	1	500	40%	200	200	6.2
High Graphic Consumer Products	2	2,500	35%	875	1,075	33.4
Meat Packers	3	2,000	32%	640	1,715	53.3
Large Low Margin Food Processors	4	3,500	30%	1,050	2,765	86.0
Large Agricultural Produce Suppliers	5	3,000	15%	450	3,215	100.0
Total		11,500		3,215	3,215	100.0

The company's efforts to improve its share of its target segments should allow it to be selective in how it deals with the least attractive segment "Large Agricultural Produce Suppliers", so that it takes only the orders that it needs to operate at full capacity. It could accomplish this by increasing its price, but there may be better alternatives like taking business only from the customers who pay on time, who are the easiest to service, or whose product mix is best for the manufacturing plant.

In any business, once the analysis is done, it will quickly become obvious that some products, market segments and pieces of geography are less attractive than others. This will provide the impetus for the development of other company strategies which could include expanding into new segments, rationalization of its production, marketing or distribution capabilities, selling some pieces of the company that do not appear to have potential, merging parts or all of the business with competitors, or acquiring other entities. In each case, the work done in the analysis will prove invaluable in developing these other strategies because the information generated in the analysis is also required for the other potential strategies. The following sections show how the information can be used to expedite the development and implementation of these other strategies.

11.1   Expansion into New Segments

The existing business will contain certain market segments, products and geographic areas which are much more profitable than the others. The reason may be related to performance versus needs, absence of constraints, lower production costs, or inferior competition, but whatever the reason, it is worth examining whether or not these advantages are transferable to other segments in which the company is not presently active. A segment is of course a combination of a product, a piece of geography, and a market segment defined by needs, so in reviewing potential new segments, it will always be preferable to be doing business in two of these dimensions, or at the least in one. This ensures that the business is not starting from scratch and that the knowledge and experience already available can be transferred to help the expansion into the new segment.

For example: if we assume that the company has product and geographic expertise and wants to expand into a new market segment, then the effort can be concentrated on doing the marketing right. This involves understanding the need profile of the target segment and the constraints that must be overcome to be successful, one of which will always be customer awareness. But, the fact that the product and geography are familiar should allow the use of some of this experience in entering the new segment, for example in providing initial sales or distribution coverage. Similarly, if it is a product or service that is new, then the existing contacts in the market should allow for very precise specifications for the new product or service to be provided to the appropriate function. Expanding geographically is probably the easiest to accomplish because the reputation established elsewhere can be used to develop awareness in the new territory and only the sales, distribution and technical service capabilities will need to be expanded. This is especially true if any existing customers have other operations in the new territory.

In any case, the simulation model will provide feedback on what to expect in terms of financial rewards for the expansion, and properly utilized, will ensure that the best options are in fact selected.

11.2   Rationalization

Obviously, some segments will not be performing as well as the majority of segments and should be considered as candidates for rationalization. However, great care must be exercised to ensure that rationalization does not have a greater negative impact than simply continuing to do business.

The greatest risk is the impact that exiting a market segment or a geographic segment will have on production costs through the loss in volume, or on distribution costs, to other segments in the same area. However, if a product is generally unprofitable, then unless production costs can be lowered or prices increased, it will probably be best to cease production. The unusual exception to this would be when a large and very profitable market segment has a high need for a complete product range. For example: it may be crucial to a plastics manufacturer that all the pigments they use have a specific and well-controlled particle size distribution. Thus, if one color or type of pigment in the range is particularly difficult to manufacture, it may nevertheless be worth maintaining because the rest of the product range is so profitable. Even then, it may be possible and more economic to outsource the difficult product rather than manufacture it. Outsourcing may also provide a solution if the problem in a particular geographic segment is related to distribution costs to one of a customer's plants in that segment and there exists a manufacturer in that area to whom production can be outsourced. In each case, the simulation model can be used to estimate the costs and benefits of rationalization.

An alternative to rationalization of a product line, if it is a self-contained business, is of course to sell it rather than close it down and this is discussed in the next section. Similarly, if a geographic area is un-economic it may make sense to sell the market share position if there are other competitors for whom the area is attractive.

11.3   Business and Asset Sales

In most large companies there are, or will be, businesses or parts of them that have little if any chance of meeting the corporate standard for profitability. They may be in a declining market, or have no hope of becoming competitive. However, they do have a share of these markets which may be attractive to other suppliers since they may need the extra volume, or they may not have the same expectations for future returns. The advantage of having done one's homework through segmentation and competitive analysis is that any business can be seen from the perspective of its competition, so that the value of its market position is taken into account, not just its asset value and operating statements, neither of which are likely to be very impressive if the business is on the potential sale list.

The competitive analysis should have made clear which of the competitors have most to gain from the removal of competitive capacity from the market, and therefore how much the business is worth to them, in terms of additional sales at their higher margins with the possibility of increasing prices as well. The ideal buyer would be one who has spare capacity or the interest and ability to invest sufficient funds in the plant in order to improve its competitiveness. From their point of view, the sales volume can be converted immediately or very quickly into significant profits. The value of the business to a potential buyer can also be calculated using the simulation model, provided that their costs can be roughly estimated, by adding the sales volume to their existing volume at current prices and developing an estimate of their incremental profit. Applying a suitable multiple to the profit number will yield a value for the transaction. Perhaps the best-known British folklore concerning this option is the "last buggy whip manufacturer", but being the last producer of just about anything is a licence to make money, at least for a while.

Of course, timing is generally very important in that even if a market is very competitive, it will look a lot better when the economy is improving than when it is in decline. The appropriate course of action is therefore to determine which businesses should be sold and to prepare a short list of potential buyers, so that when the timing is right the business can be sold quickly and at the best price. Of course to be able to do this, requires that the overall business be sufficiently profitable to allow the company to choose when it wishes to sell which in turn requires that the other parts of the business be optimized in terms of their profitability.

11.4   Acquisitions

In reviewing the various segments and determining what to do about them, there are likely to be segments which are very attractive in terms of growth and potential profitability, but which would require large expenditures on capital items, or other constraint elimination such as awareness or distribution. These should be considered sources of potential acquisition candidates.

As with all the other possible strategies, the segment analysis will provide insights into whether or not it may be possible to acquire a competitor at a reasonable price, and who are the most likely potential targets. These will be the companies with a good market share in the target segment(s), but for whom it is not a good fit because of geography, or the existence of other more attractive opportunities such as other high growth segments. They may also need to use their financial resources elsewhere. This procedure is in essence, doing the segment prioritization analysis for any potential acquisition target. Also, when the best targets have been identified, the detailed share analysis allows the value of the business to the target company to be calculated, assuming that reasonable estimates of their costs can be made.

All of this analysis allows careful preparation for an offer to be made to the target companies or the development of other strategies to encourage the target companies to sell, such as starting a price war in a segment that it is difficult for them to defend. Obviously, if the latter tactic is being considered, it is vital that the chosen company is not in a position to retaliate effectively. This too can be simulated if necessary.

11.5   Measurement and Control

Whatever plans are implemented, it is essential that tracking and control mechanisms are put in place to ensure that any planning errors, i.e. errors in estimates or assumptions, are quickly identified and corrected and the plans reworked accordingly, in addition to the normal accounting reports and controls. Frequently, because the analytical procedures that have been used in this analysis are different from those that have been used previously in the business, estimates have been used, for example, market segment sizes and market shares which are critical to the effectiveness of the plan. In these circumstances, market research should be conducted to verify the estimates and where necessary correct and rework the numbers. Depending on how long this takes, the plan may need to be revised to reflect the new reality. In any event, the key assumptions should be listed and checked periodically to ensure their accuracy, and the plan should be adjusted to reflect these differences.

CHAPTER 12   TRAINING AND WAR GAMES

One of the most useful benefits of using this segmentation and analysis process is that it is an excellent training tool. Not only does it summarize the company's business in a comprehensive and logical manner, but also makes it available to newcomers. Typically, after a few sessions it will seem as though they have been in the business for 50 years. As such, it is perfect for introducing new employees to the realities of day to day business, and best of all, it allows companies to employ people with the greatest inherent talents for the work without requiring 20 or more years of experience to even be employable in a marketing or sales capacity. It can also be used very effectively as a "War Game" training tool, allowing employees to have fun and enjoy the experience of learning the business through the process' simulation capabilities. Teams can be created to represent the various competitors and can compete realistically to be the highest profit competitor.

This is extraordinarily effective in creating not only very competent sales and marketing people, but can also help management and service personnel develop a more realistic perspective of their markets and how they need to be managed for the company to maximize its profitability. In addition, it helps develop teamwork through everyone having a common understanding of the markets they are dealing with.

The whole process works best if the sales and marketing people are involved in the development of the base data about the market's segmentation and needs analysis. In seminars introducing the process to the sales and marketing people, it is not unusual for them to say things like "it is like doing an MBA in just a few days" or "I've learned more in the past few days about our business than I learned in the previous 10 years on the job".

What differentiates the process from other training aides is that it connects everything that happens in the marketplace with the company's bottom line through the mechanism of market shares and pricing. This in turn demonstrates the inevitable causal relationships between satisfying customer needs and market shares, as well as the effect of market share on profitability.

Also, because of the emphasis on customer needs and their importance to the whole process, marketing and salespeople learn to genuinely understand and care about their customer's needs which in turn results in them providing significantly better customer service. This therefore has the added benefit of improved market performance and hence more customer satisfaction and higher market shares.

CHAPTER 13   GENERIC PRODUCT
MODELING AND PRICE

The type of analysis and ratings system that has been applied to allow the simulation of markets can also be applied to the evaluation of generic products. The essential difference between the two is that the market analysis was concerned with brand segment shares, whereas the generic product evaluation deals with function and how well each technology performs a function from the point of view of each market segment.

For example: if we consider different ways of getting from A to B on land, we might start with walking as being the slowest, then would come cycling or other wheeled and human propelled technologies like roller blades, then railway trains, then cars, and finally aeroplanes. However, before tackling that relatively complex analysis, we will revert back to the exercise book example, to illustrate the differences in the brand and generic product analysis. The different types of exercise book might be stapled or saddle stitched, coil bound, glued, stitched or perfect bound. In the school board market segment example, we looked at stapled exercise books by brand only because the need for a low price was so dominant.

If we assume that the market segment is once again school boards, then we can use the segment need weights from Table 20 on page 54, and rate each type of exercise book relative to these need weights.

TABLE 25

SCHOOL BOOKS
GENERIC COMPETITIVE ADVANTAGE

Needs	Weights	Stapled	Coil Bound	Glued	Stitched	Perfect Bound
Delivery Service	100	100	50	80	65	40
Legibility	80	80	80	80	80	80
Strength	70	50	60	40	60	70
Fixed Price	60	60	60	60	55	40
Administration	40	40	25	40	30	20
Low Price	200	200	50	140	120	50
Total Ratings	550	530	275	440	410	260
Shares (%)		27.7	14.4	23.0	21.4	13.6

As expcted, the shares of the other books are smaller by comparison. However, because of the wide variety of uses for exercise books in the other market segments like university students, teachers, professionals and authors, the need profiles will be completely different and there will be further subsegments within each of these groups.

Reverting back to the transportation example, each of the available forms of transportation has its own advantages and disadvantages that determine their shares of various market segments. To illustrate how this can be done, we will analyze a market segment for land transportation. One market with a variety of segments is the commuter market. Four of these segments might be as follows:

1. The minimum time segment
2. The economy segment
3. The environmental segment
4. The convenience segment

The need profiles of each of these might consider the following needs:

- Door to door time
- Total cost
- Convenience
- Reliability
- Health
- Environmental impact
- Utility i.e. the ability to do other things and/or transport things like luggage during the commute time
- Ease of communication

If we apply the appropriate need weights to each segment, then we should be able to estimate what the market share of each type of transportation would be for a particular market segment, within a particular piece of geography. Obviously, we will need to know what the total traffic flow is from that piece of geography to, say, the downtown core, because that represents the total market size and the sizes of each segment, all of which can be estimated initially and refined later if appropriate. We will also need to know the average cost and the average times for the area for the journey to and from work, in order to rate the cost and time needs properly.

The need profiles of the four segments might look as follows in Table 26. Most of these needs are self-explanatory, but Utility is used as a measure of capacity to carry anything in addition to a body e.g. a briefcase or other paraphernalia.

TABLE 26

COMMUTER SEGMENT NEED PROFILES

Needs	Minimum	Economy	Environment	Convenience
	Time			
Time	100	30	20	60
Convenience	50	30	10	100
Reliability	40	40	50	60
Health	30	5	70	40
Environment	5	5	100	5
Utility	15	25	5	15
Communication	40	10	10	30
Non-price Total	300	145	265	310
Price	100	200	100	80

When it comes to measuring price sensitivity, we first identify the possible means of transportation and define the geographic area in which our segments live and the place to which they are travelling. With respect to the geography, obviously the larger the areas chosen are, the less accurate the price sensitivity measures will be and the less accurate the shares will be. However, for illustrative purposes, we can assume that the price weights are approximately as shown above.

Having established the need profiles of the different segments, we now need to identify the possible means of transportation which will probably include the following: walk, cycle, motorbike, car, public transportation, taxi or Uber. The most intriguing segment is probably environmental, and the competitive profiles might look as shown below in Table 27.

TABLE 27

ENVIRONMENTAL COMMUTER COMPETITIVE PERFORMANCE

Needs	Need Weight	Walk	Bicycle	Motorbike	Car	Public Transport	Taxi	Uber
Time	20	5	15	20	20	10	20	20
Convenience	20	15	15	15	20	10	20	20
Reliability	50	40	40	35	45	35	40	40
Health	70	70	65	20	30	20	30	30
Environment	100	100	100	50	40	50	40	40
Utility	30	10	10	15	30	10	25	25
Communication	10	10	0	0	5	5	10	10
Non-Price Total	285	250	245	155	190	145	185	185
Price	100	100	90	40	15	30	10	15

The numbers shown above are just guestimates, the purpose being to illustrate how the analysis would be done when realistic data is available. This type of analysis would be invaluable to city transportation planning departments in planning traffic flows, infrastructure and service capabilities.

While the Marketing Matters Methodology is applicable to generic products and services, the complexities are such that the price relationship derived for use with branded product market segments will almost certainly not work as well and further work is needed to refine its use in particular applications.

The process can also be applied to the evaluation of new products by identifying all the products with which the new product is expected to compete and segmenting the market based on product function, and of course customer needs. For example: if the new product is a small, highly efficient two-person helicopter, it could be evaluated relative to the other commuter options using the segments already identified.

www.ingramcontent.com/pod-product-compliance
Lightning Source LLC
Chambersburg PA
CBHW030008190526
45157CB00014B/1092